D1215846

Power Multi-Level Marketing

Power Multi-Level Marketing

by

Mark Yarnell

and

Rene Reid Yarnell

QUANTUM LEAP

Reno, Nevada

U.S.A.

First Printing/ September 1988
First Revised Edition/ May 1993
Second Revised Edition / October 1995

0 9 8 7 6 5 4 3 2 1

ISBN 1-883599-06-7

Previous editions published by
MDY Publications, Inc.
ISBN 0-882059-06-9
QUANTUM LEAP
ISBN 1-883599-01-6

Published by **Quantum Leap**
4900 Neeser Lane
Reno, Nevada 89509

Printed in the United States of America

Typesetting by Denise Bevard

This book is dedicated to the one percent of people all over the world who, by entering Multi-Level Marketing and exiting the rat race, demonstrate that there are still a few individuals left with the common sense to come in out of the rain.

A SPECIAL NOTE OF GRATITUDE:

To *Doug Duwe*—for loaning us enough money to start our career in Nu Skin and to pay our bills for the first four months.
Thanks Doug.

To *Richard and Carol Kall*—who graciously took us under their wings and taught us the fundamentals of MLM.
Thanks Richard and Carol.

To the *management and office staff of Nu Skin International*—who have provided the vision and the structure to make it all possible.
Thanks Nu Skin.

To *our entire downline*—whose untiring efforts have allowed us to achieve financial freedom.
Thanks folks.

To *Paul Zane Pilzer* for trusting us to coauthor the monumental book, *Should You Quit Before You're Fired?*
Thanks Paul.

Finally, thanks to the *twenty-five MLM giants* from the five big networking companies for your straightforward remarks during the interview process and formulation of this book.
Thanks folks.

Power Multi-Level Marketing

Contents

Preface

I am saddened by the handful of books written about Network Marketing which have totally misled people. Many of the authors have jumped from company to company and, in an attempt to find the perfect "get rich quick scheme," led countless individuals down a path of certain failure. The only way to achieve lasting results in Multi-Level Marketing is to find a solvent, long-term company, work very hard, and remain loyal to that company. Next, you must act professionally.

There is nothing professional about deceptively inviting people to a dinner party and then rolling out a blackboard and drawing circles. Nor can you hope to recruit high caliber associates drawing diagrams on a napkin while sitting in a bar or restaurant. And the idea that all you need to do is find three or four quality people and help them become successful before finding others is pure malarkey. So is the concept of weekly "pump up" meetings with flag waving, marching music, and three or four mediocre speakers. Nor can you ever hope to succeed by signing up your friends or relatives, then expect to just sit back and watch your group grow.

These and other equally absurd notions have been promulgated by individuals who are only out to sell millions of books. They totally mislead innocent people who earnestly seek an exit from the rat race.

If you want to earn over $50,000 per month in MLM, you must know how to use the telephone, excite your friends, conduct a powerful recruiting meeting; you must know how to sponsor a large front line and what to do with all those people once you've gotten them. Later you'll want to know how to make cold calls and generate more leads. It is critical that you understand the difference between a matrix and a breakaway system. And, because the vast majority of all companies fail in the first year or two, you need to know what causes them to fail and how to avoid such companies. Above all else, you better have tremendously consumable and highly unique products or services and know how to retail them. Ideally, MLM is about redirected spending not behavioral modification. This book provides all the information regarding these subjects and dozens of others.

You wouldn't launch a boat and sail toward a distant coast without a navigational chart. And you certainly shouldn't launch a new career, whether full or part time, without a guide. Let me guide you through the waters of Multi-Level Marketing because about one thing I am absolutely certain: If financial freedom and peace of mind are your intended destinations, I know the way.

My wife and I were proud to accept the 1993 MLM Leadership Award and would hereby like to thank our downline for making us look good.

I'd also like to thank the editors of *Success* magazine for quoting me in their March 1993 edition and subsequently asking me to contribute monthly columns, thus sustaining the credibility of our opinions on MLM.

Mark Yarnell
May 1993

Part I

The Philosophy of
Multi-Level Marketing

Introduction

This book addresses the exploding phenomenon of Multi-Level Marketing, also known as Network Marketing and Network Distribution. It has three parts. *Part One* explains some of our philosophy of Multi-Level Marketing (MLM) including the importance of goal setting. It also describes a nearly foolproof method for choosing the right Network Marketing company.

The next two parts are the real meat—the how-tos of becoming a successful Network Marketer. *Part Two* concerns full-time power Multi-Level Marketing. *Part Three* deals with how to do MLM part-time.

The Two Paths to MLM Success

Why treat full-time and part-time Multi-Level Marketing separately? Because there are two distinct and separate ways to approach MLM, depending entirely on what you want to achieve.

The person who wants to make $10,000 to $200,000 a month, must become a *power Multi-Level Marketer.* This person with the high dollar goal must plunge into an MLM venture wholeheartedly as his life's work to ensure success. The person who cares only about an extra $500 or $600 a month, or who can't afford to quit his or her job at first, will start *part-time*. There is a world of difference between the two approaches, without making any value judgment as to your choice. If you haven't yet decided the direction you want to take, then the information in this book will explain what it takes to succeed with either approach.

There are other good reasons for discussing both methods in the same book. One is that, though they are two entirely unique approaches, both lead to success in the same industry. Another is that some requirements for professionalism—such as selecting the right company and succeeding without deception—apply to part-time MLM as well as full-time. Also, there are enough contacts among both types of people in MLM that it serves us all to know the needs of both. For example, power Network Marketers will have part-timers in their large organizations and some part-timers, having achieved income replacement, will break out and become power Marketers.

Finally, you may encounter a lot of deceptive and erroneous information written about what it takes to succeed in MLM. The information espoused by many is presented as if there were only one way, for both types of people—the part-timer and the power Marketer—to succeed. For example, one author of MLM books contends that the one way to succeed in MLM is to sign up four or five people, stop recruiting, help the four or five on the road to success, then sign up four or five more when that is accomplished. While that may have some merit for a part-timer, it is no way to succeed as a big time Network Marketer. When people surface on any level who have tremendous potential, work with them. But spend most of your time recruiting front line Distributors! Remember these three magic words: GO WIDE FAST! This must be the philosophy of a Power Marketer.

The Great Deception

It is difficult to know whether deceptive books are deliberately misleading or just a result of ignorance. But it is clear that they can give a serious black-eye to the industry, and often end up alienating a large number of potential Network Marketers. It does seem that the deceptions by several authors are monetarily motivated. Eighty-five percent of the people in MLM are part-timers, and authors, for the sake of selling more books, direct the information to those people in that category. The problem is that the deceivers often use the big checks earned by the fifteen percent who are power Marketers as bait to lure part-timers into the industry. We don't believe that's fair.

It does not serve you, us, or the industry to tell a person to use part-time techniques to earn the high-dollar rewards of a power Multi-Level Marketer. The part-timer, armed only with part-timer methods but recruited with the promise of full-time rewards, will become disenchanted with, and ultimately disenfranchised from, MLM. Then we have lost a valuable and necessary person in the industry, and have created negative word-of-mouth advertising: the *former* part-time Network Marketer who says, "They told me I could earn $20,000 a month, but it was a scam. There was no way to earn more than $600 a month." Of course, he didn't know what he was getting into, and he was never really taught how some people were making the truly big money.

What makes this book unique is that it is the first to truly describe how to become a power Multi-Level Marketer and how to draw the distinction between power MLM and part-time MLM so people can understand what it takes to succeed on either path.

The Big Difference Between Power and Part-Time MLM

One distinction between power and part-time MLM makes a world of difference in approach, income, and time spent. The distinction is whether you recruit or sell.

Although the power Marketer is concerned with representing excellent products and seeing that they get sold, his or her focus is on recruiting, training, and building a huge organization of people. In *Part Two*, we explain how to do this.

Some part-timers are concerned with marketing a retail line of products and building a small downline. The part-timer will not get rich doing this, but he or she can still achieve success. *Part Three* explains how to do this. Other part-timers put most of their energy into building an organization, but because of time constraints, will do so at a slower pace than the full-timers. Once they have replaced their incomes, professional part-timers will often quit their jobs to pursue the power MLM approach. It is recommended that these part-time organization builders generally follow the guidelines for a power Marketer in *Part Two* as opposed to the part-time approach of *Part Three*.

But understand this from the beginning: *The only sure way to get rich in Multi-Level Marketing is to build a huge organization.* It's all a numbers game and that's the bottom line.

A Character Sketch of the Power Network Marketer

It is not our intention to attempt to make stereotypical generalizations about people who become power Multi-Level Marketers. We have seen many types of people, from corporate execs to housewives, who plunge into MLM full-time at the beginning. However, the unemployed, under employed, and retired people who have taken this bold step usually do so only after a stint as a part-timer.

The typical person who dives into power MLM is one who

is driven and can see the big picture. They are frequently persons who are solidly in the rat race, in fact are in a position to be among the winners of that race. They are often very successful. Yet the problem they face is that they still find they are not really happy. Still others have the capability for success but learn about this industry at a time when they are down on their luck, or have never really been given the opportunity to explore their potential with no limits placed on them.

For two years, Mark served as the stress management director for the largest medical-sports complex in Austin, Texas. He became acquainted with numerous high-level, successful individuals from Texas, Oklahoma, Arkansas, and Louisiana who were under stress.

These people came to the clinic seeking ways to relieve ulcers, spastic colons, anxiety attacks, heart palpitations, and other stress-induced ailments. After doctors did what they could to solve the physiological problems, they would send the people to him for biofeedback training and other methods to relax and relieve stress. What became increasingly clear was that many of the people who achieve success find that the view from the top isn't nearly so attractive as they had anticipated. One executive V.P. from a major Houston firm described his business this way:

"When I go downtown to work every day, I look up at the skyscrapers and all the offices look just like drawers shoved into cabinets. I look up and see that all those poor people are just shoved into drawers like socks. And even though my drawer is near the top, I'm still just an old sock or piece of paper shoved into a drawer."

Typically, these people suffer, as this man did, from sexual dysfunction, or have children on drugs, or they never can take a vacation on a regular basis. They may work sixty-hour weeks, fight butt-numbing, nerve-shattering traffic daily, and struggle to keep an avalanche of paper from smothering them.

And often, when these people are first shown a graphic illustration of what can happen through MLM, they abandon all ties to traditional business and plunge head first into MLM trying to achieve happy success.

A short definition of the typical power Multi-Level Marketer is this: He or she is a person who is already in or previously served in a position of success but who realizes that through duplication of effort—through people in the downline—he or she can not only achieve significant passive, residual income, but also can create a tremendous amount of free time in which to enjoy it.

The Advantages of MLM

Whether you choose the power or the part-time path is irrelevant so long as you understand that there are definite and distinctly different ways to be successful at both. Regardless of which you choose, if you approach it correctly, MLM will provide you with an escape from the traditional business dilemmas which plague those people we described: no boss, no employees, no overhead, no payroll, no accounts receivable, no computer downtime.

Besides the financial rewards and the time to enjoy them, there is no other industry we know which encourages subordinates to rise above superiors with their full blessing. Competition is channeled to make everyone in the organization do as well as possible because everyone upline benefits if everyone downline does well. No dog-eat-dog. It's a wonderful notion.

MLM is the last bastion of free enterprise where each person's rewards are equal to his efforts with no ceiling on income. It is an industry where the seemingly average individual is free to use his ability to pull himself out of his predicament. You are free to work as hard as you want.

You make more meaningful friendships in a month in MLM than most people make in an entire lifetime. Some of us are even fortunate enough to find our soul mates in this industry. We did. MLM is truly a panacea because while it allows people to reap huge rewards, it also allows them to have peace and fulfillment. After all, people do not work for bread alone.

Finally, MLM is here to stay. It has a long history of success going back two thousand years ago when a man in his early thirties began his ministry based solely on the principles of Network Marketing.

Think about it closely. That young man went out and got twelve people on his frontline. He warned those twelve that as they went out to recruit others into their system, they were going to be rejected. He said to them that when they faced rejection they should just shake the dust off their feet and move on.

Interestingly, when he got into a tight spot and was subjected to horrible rejection, some of the twelve were unwilling to admit their association with him; one even betrayed him. As a result, he lost his life.

Nevertheless, following the sound principles of Network Marketing—recruiting and training other individuals—in the last two thousand years, he and his followers have captured a huge chunk of the world market share. We call it Christianity.

Multi-Level Marketing is here to stay.

Do read the whole book. For those choosing the power path, *Part Three* will help you understand the needs of the part-timers in your downline. For part-timers, the power MLM section will be invaluable to you if you eventually decide to choose the power MLM approach. You will also be able to see what it truly takes to make the big money in MLM.

Don't be confused as you read the different sections about

how to succeed. We make no value judgments. We do not believe that one approach is better than the other. It just happens that there is one way to be a power Network Marketer and another to be a successful part-timer.

We are on the brink of a very important breakthrough in Network Marketing. Only now are people beginning to discover the sophistication of this business. But the key to its power is in its simplicity. The more you create a business that can be easily duplicated, the more success you and those you recruit will experience. At the time of this writing we are still teaching the only M.B.A.-level college certification course in our industry's 40-year history. And in our course even Dr. Charles King, noted Harvard Ph.D., makes duplication the central thesis of his module on strategic planning.

Don't let one or two negatives sidetrack you. Commit to this business for two or three years, and no matter what happens, don't give up! Frequently, we've seen people give up after the first three months, just at a time when they know only enough about MLM to be dangerous. Doctors and lawyers spend years and years in training before they reach even a modicum of success. You can do it in a much shorter time than they. A close friend of ours is a pediatric cardiologist who went to school 9 years longer than Mark to end up earning annually what we earn in a month. But it did takes us over five years of hard work to reach this level of achievement.

Chapter 1

The Impact of
Multi-Level Marketing

Various numbers have been used to estimate over the past decade how many new millionaires throughout the United States, Asia and Europe have made their money in Multi-Level Marketing. Whatever the current number, it is substantial. It is perhaps the most viable, productive, and high-integrity business in the entire arena of free enterprise in which really big money can be made.

This book is a practical guide to recruiting, training, and retailing your way to MLM success. It is more than that, though. It is also a carefully thought-out approach to the overall philosophy of MLM and its evolution in the world of free enterprise. We think it's important for you to know what you are getting into when you become a part of this industry. Why is MLM so different from traditional business, and how did it become the last bastion of free enterprise?

The evolution of free world economics has led us into a confusing melee of soaring prices and daily revelations of respected people in traditional business who have cheated their friends and associates. To better understand the current economic picture, in the U.S., Europe and Asia, you will want to read, *Should You Quit Before You're Fired*, by Paul Pilzer. We wrote the forward, conclusion and commentaries for Professor Pilzer and learned a great deal about economics from him.

It is a brave new world where we pay double the value of products because of parasitic middlemen between producers and consumers. For example, when you purchase a soft drink, you also pay for a Madison Avenue PR firm, a fleet of trucks, a rack or freezer, a series of store employees, and bankers' interest on debt all along the way. In the case of a soft drink, you only pay a small amount. But, remember when an eight ounce cola was only a nickel? And that was not so very long ago.

Add the cumulative effects of such middlemen throughout the economy on almost every item you buy, and the result is mind boggling. Consider autos. Interest alone, up the production ladder before your purchase, is as much as forty percent of the purchase price. Twenty thousand dollars for a car means you pay $8,000 for hidden interest on the producer's debt.

So-called "reputable economists" would have us believe that the invisible adversary called "unchecked inflation" is our economy's enemy number one. True, inflation doesn't help, but a broader look at the spectrum brings to light the ill effects of the nasty, mushrooming "service industry." This "service industry" consists of advertisers, litigious lawyers, mid-management marketing analysts, debt brokering bankers—anybody who avoids producing and distributing products yet lives off the inflated value of the product.

In today's traditional business world, billions of dollars are spent on meaningless advertising campaigns even though everyone knows that the strongest form of advertising is "word-of-mouth." Year in and year out, traditional business pours billions more into middle management salaries regardless of production. "We the people" have the privilege of financing all of this.

All this nonsense isn't confined to the business world, either. I recently visited with a doctor friend who, in robust health at age fifty, left the field he loves because, "I've now accumulated enough rental property to live comfortably without having to endure the fear and financial pressure of malpractice suits and malpractice insurance." Middlemen parasites called lawyers and insurance agents skip merrily to the bank with their profits off the dedicated medical community (and each other) through their exorbitant premiums, settlements, and legal fees. But a neighborhood has lost an excellent doctor who never bargained for this scenario while in medical school. He left behind his sutures and stethoscope for a ladder and paintbrush to begin a second career in property maintenance.

Even worse, now a new parasite has entered the medical world of woe, as it eventually does in all fields—advertising—which always seeks its pound of flesh from every make-a-buck scam. With removal of advertising bans on lawyers, we now see a growing number of slick ads haranguing the masses into believing that they need legal help to get compensation for accidental injuries or errors of other professionals. It's an endless cycle. We recently saw a television ad in New York in which some ridiculous lawyer actually stated, "Even if you think you haven't been injured at work, call us for a free consultation."

Not true in Network Marketing. MLM cuts out the middlemen with a judicious broadsword. A bare minimum of people are involved in distributing the product from producer to consumer. Instead of spending billions on hackneyed, pithy jingles to persuade consumers to consume, MLM relies on the ancient, time-honored method of word-of-mouth advertising. It's a little slower, but it works without inflating the price of a product. The Network Distributor works for himself in the purest form of free enterprise: if he doesn't produce, he doesn't eat. Simple, straight-forward, leaving the product and price closer to its true value.

Because of these differences, Network Distribution has definite advantages over traditional business both for the individual who feels comfortable with his competence to work in a free atmosphere, and for consumers. And Multi-Level Marketing can be extremely lucrative. However, there is no point in glossing over some of the bad press and government raps that MLM has taken over the years. You will need to know about them, why they occur, and how to handle these objections.

There are three reasons for the bad press.

1. Network Marketing has no self-regulating body to internally address problems at a time of government deregulation.
2. The press is always out to find a juicy story that condemns an industry for isolated incidents.
3. Some people in Network Marketing are unethical in the way they conduct their business.

MLM has no watchdog associations to regulate violators who go beyond legal Networking limits as interpreted by the provincial regulatory bodies. Anyone with a minimum of money and brains can launch a company and push it nationwide overnight. The challenge is sustaining it.

In any industry where people can realize quick, big money, charlatans and carnival barkers abound. Consider the investment industry. Now, imagine if such an industry didn't have any self-regulation. It's bad enough when industries are regulated, but, without self-regulation, industries always run the risk of being shut down by some branch of government. Now, with deregulation fashionable, the government doesn't step in until a problem has become acute and many people have been hurt.

Along with the problems in any industry, the press hops in with both feet. An over zealous journalist, always happy to "expose" negatives, picks up the story of an isolated indiscretion and portrays the activity as systemic to the industry. In their eagerness to right a wrong, to win that Pulitzer, they fail to explore the actual workings of the industry. The result is erroneous information through association.

We believe Network Marketing needs a self-regulating and information body. Although the Direct Selling Association in Washington, D.C. has done their best to oversee this industry, they are much more focused (as their name clearly proves) on Direct Selling Companies. I think they would probably like to see most MLM companies just "go away." Eventually we will have our own legitimate organization. Every industry needs a way to intercede between government and itself before problems get out of control and strong punitive measures by the government become necessary. Every industry needs the strength and wherewithal to respond to erroneous information and to explain how an isolated illegal act isn't common to the industry.

Realistically, we can't make that happen and neither can you. Not yet, anyway, but we're working on it. More important to us, though, is to understand that there is a right way and wrong way to do Multi-Level Marketing. Do it the right way, and you won't need to worry about press or the regulators. All you need are some professional guidelines.

This book provides those guidelines. If you follow them and don't try to reinvent the wheel, you will succeed.

Just one more preliminary note. The age-old adage, "You will get out of this exactly what you put into it," holds truer for Network Marketing than any other industry. People who are looking for get-rich-quick schemes will become disillusioned in a hurry because the companies that use that hook as a recruiting inducement are the most likely to fail in the first year or two. That is the wrong way to do MLM. Conversely, those who do want to do MLM the right way, to work diligently in order to provide themselves and their families with financial stability, will do so faster and with substantially less risk than in any other field. And those who also are extremely skilled at communications and are highly motivated to succeed can expect incomes of staggering proportions.

Those who see Network Marketing as a vehicle to use their financial and time freedom for higher purposes—goals bigger than themselves—will generally find it easier to stay focused in this business. With their sights set on a goal to transform their success toward, in some way, making a difference in the world, their success is more imminent.

Chapter 2

Selecting the
Right Company

Before marrying Rene, in one short year I worked very diligently to become one of the most successful Network Marketing executives in America. However, my success didn't really come overnight. My approach significantly differs from many who have jumped into multi-level opportunities without careful consideration, gambling their fortunes and their families' futures. Luckily I had a great coach named Richard Kall, and I had done my due diligence.

It took me nine long years to search out the marketplace for the right company to represent—one which offered me the latitude to use my skills in signing up some of the most high-powered professional people while not running the risk of being shut down after the first six months by some zealous state attorney general for operating a pyramid scam. Of course, I was doing other things during those nine years—delivering keynote speeches to large conventions, consulting Fortune 500 companies, and pastoring churches. However, like others in Texas, the state economy finally got me.

The concept of Multi-Level Marketing—the low overhead, the freedom to use one's professional abilities to the fullest, and financial rewards for what is essentially word-of-mouth advertising—had always appealed to me. Yet often, like so many of you, when I was approached by someone to sign up for a multi-level operation, I experienced a painful little shudder during the presentation.

What was it that my little shudder was telling me? Why did I shy away from signing up? Perhaps it always sounded too much like get-rich-quick schemes. Perhaps they tried to leave the impression that a person could get something for nothing. Usually it was my perception that something was missing in a particular company's marketing plan or product.

I'm sure that I bypassed opportunities to join some good multi-level companies. There was really no way to know. But if the person making the presentation didn't know more about the company or the business side of Network Distribution than he demonstrated during the presentation, there was no way to know if that was the company's position or if it was just the unprofessional attitude of the person trying to sign me up. Either way, I couldn't take the risk. Nobody presented it right.

What I came to realize is this: Although MLM can provide huge financial rewards and freedom, and can exploit weaknesses inherent in traditional business, a person's approach to MLM must still be very professional. That's true if you are a part-timer like Rene was or if you are going to tackle it gung ho like I did.

You need specific criteria about whom you are going to sponsor and how you are going to conduct your business. During our combined 16 years, we have developed a plan and criteria for the Network Marketing business that will save you time and pain. If you follow it, you will be in a position to reap the rewards of Multi-Level Marketing without suffering all the mistakes most novices experience. You will become established in the industry with a solid footing that offers stability and security.

The first step to success in MLM is to select the right company. This doesn't just mean the "right" company for you, though that is part of it. It means a company which will be in business in two decades. This is the most important stage in your MLM trek. The criteria for selecting a good company explodes many of the myths surrounding MLM, and our plan will probably make some people in this industry unhappy. However, it will save most people headaches and vast sums of money.

Criteria for the *Perfect* Multi-Level Marketing Company

The following are criteria you should look for to determine the *perfect* multi-level company. Keep in mind that these are the ideals, and *you will rarely find a company that has all of them*.

1. The company you choose should have been in business for *at least* two years and have founders and field distributors with significant MLM experience.
2. The company's products should be unique, consumable, have mainstream American acceptability, and be reasonably priced.
3. The company should have a low distributor investment and generous return policy.
4. The company should pay *at least* three levels deep; four, five, or six levels is the ideal at four or five percent per level.
5. The company should have a qualification period to prevent the possibility of buy-ins.

6. The company should have plans for international expansion.
7. An American-based company should be a member in good standing of the U.S. Direct Selling Association.
8. The company's stockholders and investors should not also be field distributors.

Those are the ideal criteria, and should be seriously considered prior to involvement in an MLM business. Less than five out of seven should preclude anyone from participating in that particular company. You will seldom find a single company which possesses all of them. However, the first is the most important.

Most people who start an MLM corporation do so with good and meaningful intentions. They may have good products or services. They believe they can get their unique products or services out to the customer either faster or cheaper or both, through a Network Distribution organization.

But they fail to understand the essence of this industry, the very simple, yet all-encompassing nature of it's power: *The basis for MLM is word-of-mouth advertising*. And though word-of-mouth is the strongest, most reliable, and purest form of advertising, it can also work against you.

Here's what happens to many young companies. The company with a very good product hires ten experienced multi-level experts. They, in turn, put on ten more people each. Ten experienced Multi-Level Marketers can cause a company's marketing force to grow by 2,000 to 3,000 recruits each month. The result is a sales force which creates a demand that outstrips the company's ability to produce. Products get back ordered, or quality deteriorates. What began as a good word-of-mouth campaign ends with the company going down due to poor planning and an inability to keep pace.

A more sinister plot is that some people start multi-level companies with the intention of taking them into bankruptcy sometime later down the road. Principles can form a corporation and take their profits from initial fees. Within six months, without ever having to concentrate on production, they can fold the company and pocket seven or eight million dollars. We are convinced that this scenario is common. We've seen one couple start four different MLM scams in the last decade each of which went out of business in under 24 months.

Whatever the reason, the salient fact is this: *most Multi-Level Marketing companies are bankrupt in the first eighteen months*.

On the other hand, almost all companies that survive the first couple or so years, go on for eight to ten years and stay strong and solvent. It is advisable to join a company even older yet, if it is expanding into your market from another country. Corporate and field experience is an added plus. It is extremely helpful to have leaders with successful track records steering others away from the pitfalls and toward proven systems.

The second criteria—*unique and consumable products*—is absolutely critical to your long-term success if you are interested in passive residual income. Consumability is what ultimately creates time freedom.

The principle of redirected spending is critical to long-term success in our industry. You're not trying to change behavior so much as you are inviting your friends to redirect their spending on items they are using anyway. This is very effective assuming that your products are higher quality or less expensive. Then follow this by educating people about products in which behavior modification is needed. Having come to appreciate your primary products, customers will be much more receptive to trying new products which they are not accustomed to using.

If you find a company with at least one or two unique products, you will have built-in sales appeal. You have something that no one else has. Many companies that major in products such as soaps, have some unique products as well, and it thus becomes easy to modify people's behavior if they have already used your mainstream items and liked them.

Corresponding to unique products, you should make sure the company's products are highly consumable and of excellent quality. You want your customers reordering your unique products time and time again. They should be reasonably priced, mid-ranged between drug store items and expensive department store lines.

The third criteria: *a low investment and generous return policy.* There is no reason to require a major investment in a Network Distribution company. Mark turned $179.00 of borrowed capital into a multimillion dollar organization. You should not be expected to spend more than a few hundred dollars to get your business started. A company's return policy is critical. If a company does not allow its Distributors to return all products for at least a 90% refund any time in their first two to three years, you are in for problems. UPWHAGS (Unhappy People With Houses and Garages Stuffed) will do everything in their power to get their money back after purchasing large numbers of products they can't seem to sell. They will scream "pyramid" to any regulator, journalist or lawyer who will listen. Of course, it's really their own fault for attempting to buy their way in or loading up on products in order to qualify for higher commission payouts (most companies have minimum sales requirements).

One company taught its Distributors to test every piece of equipment when it arrived, supposedly to keep the customer from getting a defective product. This company also had a policy of accepting no used product for return. Everything that was tested by the Distributors, as they had been instructed, was considered used equipment and could not be returned. Such a practice is an outrage and should be reported to a local investigative body and to the Direct Sales Association.

The fourth criteria: *a payout of at least three levels deep.* Avoid companies that pay only one or two levels deep for your breakaway people. If a company limits itself in this way, then multiplying your efforts will only have a minor benefit to you.

A Network Distribution company in which you are interested must pay at least three levels deep. The ideal company pays four, five, or six levels deep at four or five percent per level.

The fifth criteria: *qualification period.* There should be a qualification period during which new Distributors are expected to sell products and learn the business before being allowed to derive an economic benefit from people in their entire organization. If a person can "buy" his way to the top of the compensation plan, that is frequently regarded as a pyramid scheme.

The sixth criteria: *plans for international expansion.* We live in a global community and great companies like Amway and Nu Skin have demonstrated that their Distributors need and deserve the massive revenues that come from foreign expansion. You should probably not join a company that can't demonstrate that they have the desire and wisdom to expand into Europe and the Pacific Rim. Growth into foreign markets can represent as much as 60-80 percent of your potential revenue.

The seventh criteria: *member of the Direct Selling Association.* One shouldn't even consider joining an American MLM company which isn't a member in good standing of the U.S. DSA. In America, this organization is extremely well-respected, carefully selects its members, and is objective in its evaluations.

The eighth criteria: *a separation between stockholders/investors and field distributors.* Although a company may be able to make this work effectively, it is generally best to make a clear distinction between a company stockholder and a field distributor. Much like the politician who feels obligated to return political favors to campaign contributors, there could emerge a false sense of loyalty to the stockholder or his/her family years down the road. Fairness is everything in Multi-Level Marketing. If it was ever perceived that preferential treatment were given to a stockholder/distributor and his/her downline, it could be the undoing of the company. Many executives have left the dog-eat-dog competitive world of Corporate America in lieu of the supportive atmosphere and level playing field of Network Marketing. Make sure that the policies and procedures of your company apply to and are equally adhered to by all company participants.

Evaluate the Management Team

Once you have determined which company has the most potential, you must determine the credentials of those who run the company and are on the management end of marketing. Check the company out with Dunn and Bradstreet or some other investigative firm. It astonishes us to see as many people as we do act as if it is some major hurdle to check on the upper management of a company. The thing to remember is that you are going into business for yourself representing their company and products. They need you and you need them. What's more, they are always looking for good recruits and an excellent sign of a good recruit is someone who is willing to research the company. From a practical perspective, you are about to enter a business where, if you do your work, you could quickly be earning six figures. What kind of a business person would you be if you didn't find out how you were going to get along with management and how they were going to support you and all the people you bring with you?

One thing you will want to ask about management people is, *"What is their past business experience?"* Focus specifically on their experience in Network Marketing. If they try to dazzle you with management positions they may have held in traditional business, avoid becoming overly impressed. My experience is that past success in traditional forms of business has little to do with success in Network Marketing. The real experts in MLM will have been involved in other successful direct-selling ventures over the years or will surround themselves with experts who have.

Other subjects you might discuss are things like how often are products back-ordered? Does the company have a trouble-shooting department? Can you review accounts readily? Are the average income earnings of each level published? Does the corporation have an experienced research and development team for the purpose of creating and evaluating new products?

In general, company management should be enthusiastic and experienced. The real expert in MLM corporate management likes to talk to a new Distributor occasionally and will understand why you, as someone considering joining the company, want to know about him and the company.

Analyze the Company's Compensation Plan

Before you get caught up in the hype and glitter of a particular company and its products, analyze the company's compensation plan and its method of payment. There are some important DOs and DON'Ts you must follow if you want long term success. In fact, a bad marketing plan could prevent you from the success you want to achieve.

Avoid matrix systems, go for a breakaway plan

This suggestion will concern some who are already a part of a matrix system, or companies that operate one. However, we don't believe that the matrix is the optimum plan for you nor will it work in the long-run. Every piece of evidence illustrates that a matrix breaks down by the time you go several levels deep.

Let us explain. A matrix limits your "frontline," the people you directly sponsor who make up the first level under you. A breakaway does not. For example, a common matrix only allows you to have four or five people you recruit positioned as your frontline. Any others you might recruit then go under the first four or five on your frontline. The problem with that is that your percentage of the take is reduced at lower levels or the deeper you go into the matrix. Worse, they can never be realistically filled. The matrix is contrary to the philosophy of MLM because a person who is active and works hard to recruit Distributors is penalized by arbitrary limits rather than rewarded for sterling performance.

In a *breakaway plan*, you can go as wide as you want, without restriction, by personally sponsoring any number of people on your frontline. We'll explain the ramifications of that as far as percentage payments and the advantages to you in more depth later.

Here is a specific example of the ill-effects of a matrix. It was described by Samuel Shapiro, a professor of statistics at Florida International University in Miami for the June 1987 issue of *Money Magazine* and concerns a matrix MLM company that sold offshore loan packages:

> "All of those entering on level nine of this particular pyramid would qualify for a thousand dollar loan, only if together they signed up the equivalent of every living soul in the United States, Canada, the Netherlands and Mexico—a total of 362.8 million people."

The point is, by the time you are sponsored into a particular matrix, in order to make a success of yourself, mathematically you may have to recruit an impossible number of people.

However, with its system of "roll-ups," a breakaway plan allows individuals to recruit as many frontline Distributors as they can or wish and ultimately benefit even if the recruits quit. We'll discuss roll-ups in more depth later.

Stay away from companies that allow people to buy their way to the top —

Some companies will allow people to reach the top levels by paying thousands of dollars. These people often purchase huge amounts of products and just stack them in the garage. The practical reason for avoiding such companies, besides the fact that in such a firm people can jump ahead of you with little effort, is that such firms are continually under investigation.

Many regulatory bodies consider a plan where people can buy their way to the top, an illegal pyramid. Ultimately the plan topples. Regulators frown on programs where wealthy people can benefit faster than others.

Some MLM companies have a system established where new Distributors have to do some retailing of products before reaching high pay scales. Such companies are in the best position to avoid regulatory and media problems.

These simple suggestions on selecting the right company will not ensure your success. They will, however, put you on the road to success and help you avoid the need to jump from company to company or experience the pitfalls that many people encounter when they enter Multi-Level Marketing.

Let's review:

- Multi-Level Marketing is a business, and you must approach it professionally.

- To choose the ideal company, judge it using these criteria, keeping in mind that few companies possess all of them:

    1. It should have been in business for at least two years and have founders and field distributors with significant MLM experience.
    2. The company should have consumable products, reasonably priced in a mid-range, at least one or two of which are unique.
    3. The company should have a low investment and generous return policy.
    4. The company should pay *at least* three levels deep; four, five, or six is the ideal at four to five percent per level.
    5. The company should have a qualification period in order to avoid the possibility of buy-ins.
    6. The company should have plans for global expansion.
    7. An American company should be a member in good standing of the U.S. Direct Selling Association.
    8. The company's stockholders and investors should not also be field distributors.

- The first criteria is the most important and must never be ignored. Most Multi-Level Marketing companies go bankrupt in the first two years.

- Word-of-mouth advertising is the key to Network Marketing. It can work for you or against you.

- Some people start MLM companies with the intention of making them bankrupt within the first few months.

- Closely check out the background of the principle stockholders.

- The company you choose should have highly consumable and excellent quality products. Redirected spending, rather than behavioral modification, is most effective in MLM.

- A company should allow its Distributors to return all unused products for at least a 90% refund for their first two to three years.

- Avoid companies that pay only one or two levels deep. Ideal companies pay four, five, or six levels deep at four or five percent.

- Growth into foreign markets can represent as much as 60-80 percent of your potential revenue.

- Determine the company's former management experience in MLM. Management in traditional forms of business does not necessarily translate into success in Network Marketing.

- Analyze the company's compensation plan.

- Make sure the company pays specific percentages at all levels.

- Stay away from companies that allow people to buy their way to the top. Some regulatory bodies consider those illegal pyramids.

- Avoid companies with matrix systems which make success mathematically impossible.

- A matrix limits the number of people on your frontline and on every subsequent level under you.

- Choose a breakaway plan where the width of the frontline is not restricted.

- Then ... GO WIDE FAST!

Chapter 3

SETTING GOALS
Creating Your Business Plan

"Goals not written down are only a wish." This is a serious business and needs to be treated as such. Goals that are written down have focus, and focus will bring them into being. What you want to achieve in your business is *your business,* but commit your plan, goals and accomplishments to writing—whether you have 5 hours or 50 hours a week to give to your new business. Then translate these goals into specific action steps.

Written goals and a written prospect list are absolutely essential for getting a new Marketing Associate started in the business. Complete these two steps yourself and insist on them being accomplished before you will continue to work with any new people that you introduce into your organization. This is a sign of commitment. The sponsor will want to be familiar with, or help formulate, the new Associate's business plan and committed goals.

Close communication is essential to keeping new Marketers on track with their goals. From time to time you may need to do some troubleshooting for your Distributor or for yourself to determine if something is going wrong and where the breakdown is:

- Approaching enough people every day about the business opportunity
- Setting the appointments
- Getting enough people to the presentations
- Closing recruits with the help of upline support
- Offering a duplicable training system

Once you determine where the problem is, make the necessary adjustments. If one lead source is not working, change to another. But one thing you can be sure of—if you work this plan and stick with it, the plan will work for you!

The stronger your sense of purpose, the greater your chance of success in this business. To help you develop a strong sense of purpose—a preeminent purpose overriding your entire life —you are encouraged to take the time to thoughtfully complete the exercise on the next page. We use this exercise as a part of our certification course in Network Marketing at the University of Illinois at Chicago. Some of our students have had phenomenal, and sometimes emotional, breakthroughs about discovering their real purpose in life. **Network Marketing is merely the vehicle to help you achieve your preeminent purpose.** The overall concept of this exercise came from the Tartaglia Mind Technologies Institute in Sylvania, Ohio. This will help you stay focused on what passionately drives you to succeed beyond material possessions. It is that strong desire that will carry you through the difficult challenges, the rejections, and the disappointments inherent in this business.

Discovering Your Preeminent Purpose

A. **Life Script**: Outline the main events of your life, including those that have led to conflict; note whether you rose above the conflict and if so how; whether any resolution was reached; pay close attention to any repetitive patterns. For example, divorce, rebellion against parents or others, circumstances surrounding schools and how far you went, repeatedly changing jobs and why, marital challenges, alcoholism.

B. **Supporting Values**: List those values that are dominant in you and which often create conflict. For example, you value honesty, tranquility, a simple life, pleasing others, loyalty, straightforwardness, genuine compassion, positive attitude.

C. **Moral Dilemma**: Note any major or recurring conflict in your life. For example, you are caught up in power and prestige, constant battles, feelings of abandonment, workaholism, alcoholism, facing situations that lack integrity.

D. Personal Transformation: Are you aware of any change in you that has enabled you to rise above the conflict or moral dilemma? If so, note that the change was *from* what *to* what. If not, how do you see the resolution coming about to make it possible for you to rise above the moral dilemma in your life? For example, something significant occurs to lead you to assume more responsibility; from seeking power and prestige to a simple, tranquil life; from constant conflicts to a spirit of cooperation.

E. Redefined Identity and Purpose: Who are you after transformation and what are you ultimately about? What do you see as your ultimate purpose in life? For example, your life is about protecting the downtrodden, standing up for what is ethical, fighting for a specific cause, an overwhelming desire to make a difference in a particular area of life.

Having defined your ultimate purpose, now go on to use the worksheets on the following pages to set your short and long term goals in writing. Then establish your specific business plan, using the medium of your MLM business, to help you achieve your goals.

GOAL SETTING WORKSHEET

For New Marketers

Date:_____

The precipitating event or cause that drives me to start my own Network Marketing business is:_____
_____

In 3 years, I see myself living (where, how?)_____
_____ **with the freedom to** (do what?) _____ **and with an income of $**_____ **as a result of my Network Marketing business.**

In 2 years, I see myself living _____
with the freedom to _____
and with an income of $_____ **as a result of my Network Marketing business.**

In 1 year, I see myself living _____
with the freedom to_____
and with an income of $_____ **as a result of my Network Marketing business.**

Specific Short Term Goals:

In order to attain my one year goal, I will achieve _____ level in my Company. (Inquire about the most recent average earnings. Base your goal on actual accomplishments of others according to the compensation plan paid out.) I will notify the Company of my intent to pursue leadership status by submitting a letter of intent in the month of _____, 199__.

Business Plan

The following is a suggestion for establishing a yearly business plan that, if adhered to consistently, should bring the desired results. However, this is not a set guarantee as you need to allow for certain intangibles: positive attitude, credibility, communication skills, rapport with your contacts, etc. Remember, base your goal of achievement level on actual proven financial track records of successful people in the company. Asking for this information is also a good way to do your due diligence on the company. Set your sights on the highest leadership level (e.g., Emerald Executive, Regional Director, Diamond Breakaway) that you are targeting the first year in order to achieve your financial goals.

To achieve _____ level in my business, I will commit to the following:

I will allocate _____ hours a day to my business. Of this time, I will spend _____ hours per day (70 to 80% of my time) prospecting for new Network Marketers.

CREATING VOLUME WITHIN MY ORGANIZATION:

No one makes any money in Network Marketing unless product is being ordered. The following first year goal setting is necessary both for those part-timers committed solely to retail selling as well as those who are committed to building a network of Marketers:

I commit to creating a wholesale volume of $_____ ^A ¯**in sales each month.** Of this volume, my family and I will personally use $_____. Therefore, I will retail the balance of this volume $_____ for which I will be compensated $_____ in profits. To achieve this, I commit to the following:

Formula: Base your estimates on actual experience of someone's upline who has a successful and proven track record.

1. In order to retail $_____$ [A] wholesale volume, I will produce _____ [B] customers each month who average $50 each of wholesale volume orders. (Divide 50 into the wholesale volume you set as a goal. The customers retail purchase will be 30 to 50% more than this amount.)

2. This means I will average _____ [C] new customers each week. (Divide the number of customers by 4.)

3. In order to create this number of customers each week, I will show the product or give samples to _____ [D] people. (It takes an average of 3 showings to result in 1 customer. Multiply the number of customers[C] by 3.)

4. In order to show or give samples to this many people, I will contact ___ [E] people per week about the products. (It takes an average of 2 contacts to result in 1 who will look at or try the product. Multiply the number of people approached [D] by 2.)

BUILDING DISTRIBUTORS IN MY ORGANIZATION:

Formula: It will take an average of 2 Marketers pursuing a Breakaway position to create one stable leader. In order to generate _____ Executives on my front line in one year, I need to create a total of _____[1] who are willing to strive for this. (Multiply number of Leaders wanted by 2)

Formula: Sponsor an average of 6 Associates to generate one who will pursue a Leadership position this year. I'll sponsor _____[2] new Associates this year. (Multiply number of Leaders[1] by 6.)

Formula: Present the opportunity to an average of 5 people in your warm market, 7.5 in your warm/cold, and 10 in your completely cold market in order to sponsor one new Marketer.

I will make a presentation or give information to _____ [3] people. (Multiply number of Associates[2] by 5, 7.5, or 10, depending on the how well you know your prospects.)

Formula: Prospect an average of 5 people in your warm market, 10 in your warm/cold market and 15 in your completely cold market in order to get one to a presentation (or, if long-distance, to seriously look at your multimedia packet).

I will prospect a total of _____ [4] people in the first year. (Multiply the number of people to whom you are making presentations[3] by 5, 10 or 15, depending on how well you know your prospects.)

Formula: Divide your total number of prospects[4] by 12 (or the number of months needed to attain your goal) to see how many prospects you must contact per month. Divide that number by 4.3 to determine how many prospects you need to call on weekly. Divide that number again by the number of days per week you plan to prospect for a daily average.

I will prospect _____ [5] people per week in order to achieve my goal of creating the determined number of leaders on my front line. That works out to _____ [5] people per day that I will talk to about this business opportunity.

The numbers are staggering, but this is the hard truth about Network Marketing. You will sift through a vast number of people in order to find the gold nuggets. It is a numbers game. Those who enter into this business understanding this are less shocked by the numbers they go through in order to find the real leaders. The more connected you are to people who are in turn well connected to leaders whose time is right for this kind of business, the better your odds. The key is not to take rejection personally, and commit to prospecting huge numbers of people the first two to three years in this business. Don't get side-tracked into too much management of your people, that you let up on your commitment to prospect new people daily.

Now go on to study the information on **Establishing a Business Plan** so you can determine specific sources of your prospecting leads.

ESTABLISHING A BUSINESS PLAN

As you get started and begin to establish your business plan, you will need to choose the recruiting methods that are the most appropriate for you to build your business. The following is a list in order of priority. Number one is far more effective than number eight.

1. **Build a Prospect list:** This is not only the first but by far the most important way to begin by working through your center of influence. If you are over the age of 30, you know 2,000 people on a first name basis. Write them all down. Remember, do not qualify your prospects.

2. **Referral system:** Reach out to people with whom your friends and contacts suggest you get in contact. For those who are reluctant to get into business, offer to work their leads for them. If some of their people choose to enroll, the person who referred them will seriously reconsider joining your team.

3. **Lifestyling:** Go about your normal day (work, health club, bank, grocery store, day care, lunch with friends, seeing clients, working with customers, car repair, golf or tennis), and, taking only seconds at a strategic moment, plant a seed about your business opportunity. Never stop to give detailed information at this point. Simply exchange business cards, or better yet, ask permission to contact them at a specific time (get their phone number).

4. **Utilize clientele or organization lists:** You may also purchase mail lists to which you have access, e.g., former clients, teachers, real estate agents, sales organizations, clubs, etc. All mailings should be a provocative statement about time freedom and financial independence.

5. **Run newspaper ads:** Advertise on Sunday in the sales section stressing financial independence/time freedom.

6. **Cold calling on business people:** Take time each day to go where business people gather; walk up to them and prospect them by asking a provocative question. Or generate your own leads from home by selecting a category in the yellow pages of your phone book or from a reference book at your local library (e.g., stockbrokers, mortgage brokers, savings and loan agencies, advertising agencies). Call them indicating that we have many successful people who are blending their business with ours to increase their present income; offer to have your runner (which may be you!) drop off some information.

7. **Speaking engagements to clubs and organizations:** Arrange for you or your upline to speak to business and community-minded groups about the concept of Network Marketing—not specifically about your company—with all the forces driving its success in today's market.

8. **Business Opportunity card pass out:** Write a provocative statement on a generic business card, handing out or, where permitted, passing out the cards appropriately (airports, restaurants, fairs, and convention centers—wherever people are gathered). Have the card refer the person back to your local voice mail system. Then follow up with a phone call and an invitation to a presentation. This approach takes incredible numbers to be effective.

Based on this outline for creating a business plan, choose those that will give you the greatest chance of success for building your business and continue your **Goal Setting Worksheet**.

Commitment: In order to show the opportunity to the number of contacts daily/weekly and meet the goals I have set for myself, I will prospect people according to the following daily/weekly (select one) business plan:

(1) calling _____ people from my prospect list

(2) generating _____ leads through referrals

(3) contacting _____ people through lifestyling

(4) calling _____ from a client/organizational list

(5) generating _____ leads through newspaper ads

(6) generating _____ leads by calling on business people (either phone or personal contact)

(7) generating _____ leads through speaking engagements

(8) generating _____ leads through business opportunity cards/flyers.
(see formula below)

Formula: To create a law of average for generating leads through cards/flyers, random pass outs must be done in very large numbers: 1200 flyers / opportunity cards = 24 phone responses = 12-15 leads = 1 Distributor.

If I am using business opportunity cards or flyers as part of my means to generate contacts, I am committed to passing out cards/flyers weekly in order to generate _____ leads.

Adding up all 8 numbers above, this means I will prospect a total of _____ [5] people daily/weekly (matches your figure [5] from the worksheet on page 38).

Study the example of a **Daily Action Plan** and then transfer the information from this worksheet to the commitment sheet at the end of this chapter.

Example of a Daily Action Plan

Plan A: Working through the opportunity.

The following is an example of an Action Plan for Marketing Associates on a two to three year road to a top leadership position . This assumes you are putting in long hours and working in a warm to lukewarm market. Statistics vary greatly depending upon the strength of your relationships with your prospects and your style of presenting this opportunity to them. Also modify your Daily Action Plan according to personal variables and the goals you set for yourself. Most new Associates are astounded at the large numbers of people you must sift through in order to find the right fit of people with your opportunity. It is critical that you understand what a numbers game this business is. The following plan is realistic. **If you want to go faster, and achieve a leadership position in 12-18 months, increase the number of people you prospect to 30 a day.**

If you choose to lower the numbers of people you approach in the first step, remember that you must also adjust your goals by extending the number of years out proportionately in which you plan to achieve this leadership level. If you are approaching 8 to 10 people a day, for most Marketers, it will take twice as long, perhaps 4 to 5 years, to achieve the desired leadership position and income level. If you approach 4 to 5 people a day, it could take 8 to 10 years. If you do less than that....

A. **Talk to 15 to 20 people per day about the financial and time freedom possible through Network Marketing.** We think of Network Marketing as a numbers game. Whoever talks to the most people wins. It is recommended that you not go into detail at this first stage. Don't mention the name of your company or the product line yet. Stress the financial and time freedom: (1) If you want to find a way out of the rat race, (2) If you want to find a reasonable alternative to replace the fading myth of government subsidized retirement programs, (3) If you want a residual-type income that can provide security for you and your family, (4) If you want to have not only enough money but the time to enjoy it, (5) If you want to take charge of your life ... then we need to talk.

B. **Set appointments with those prospects who showed interest.** Call and invite the prospect to your home (or arrange to send a multimedia packet if long-distance). Arrange a time, give directions, and avoid the temptation to say too much. A rule of thumb for cold prospecting: four out of 15 people, or about 25% of those you prospect will *agree* to come to the presentation, and 1 out of 2 to 3 of them *will actually follow through.* These statistics will be higher in your warm market.

C. **Make presentations to 10-15 people per week.** The most effective presentation is to a small group in your home or other similar place where you have the best chance of showing others how much excitement and fulfillment this opportunity could bring to their lives. This is highly duplicable and can be done as frequently as you wish without the burden of expensive overhead. Placing audio/video packets as a method of prospecting is especially good for long-distance recruiting and will leverage your time. It sifts through the prospects so that you can spend your personal time on the phone or in private presentations with those who are especially interested.

D. **Use upline support for closing.** People need to hear about the opportunity and products from more than one source. Let your sponsor help close your strongest contacts. Three-way conference calls or a direct call from your prospect to someone in your upline are excellent closing methods. This is especially true when you are new in the business and don't know all the answers. You don't want to practice your presentation on your top prospects. You want someone else (preferably with a track record) to help close prospects until you achieve a leadership position. At that time you take over the closing calls for your downline.

E. **Approach three retail customers per week.** This can be done through the business presentation. Those who say *no* to the business opportunity frequently say *yes* to the products. Retailing is an essential component of this business. Each of us needs to build a small customer base in order to duplicate the process and build a large successful organization.

F. **Sponsor an average of 5-10 new Associates each month.** Your closing ratios will vary greatly depending on many factors, but strive to sponsor at least two new Associates each week. This will keep you from arriving at the end of the month still needing to complete your sponsoring goal. Until you reach the leadership level toward which you are striving, *never stop building your front line*. And that means that you must never stop prospecting. Prospect, prospect, prospect every day.

Plan B: Working through the product.

The following is an example of an Action Plan for part-time Distributors who would prefer to commit fewer hours to their business, want to use the products and purchase them at wholesale prices, build a retail customer base, and gradually enroll others into the program.

A. **Talk to 5 people per day about the product line.** Share your enthusiasm and personal results from using the products. Ask permission to follow up.

B. **Show the product line to 15 people per week.** This can be done through a small group presentation in your home, sharing information/samples or holding a professional clinic.

C. **Create 5 customers per week.** If your product is a more expensive item or service, this number will be smaller but the return to you should be larger. Strive to get the order from your prospective customers and to get product delivered promptly.

D. **Service your existing customers, while continuing to prospect for new ones.** Where appropriate, offer special programs to your customers based on availability, e.g., ordering through a toll-free number or having the product sent through an automatic delivery program.

E. Ask for Referrals from your customers once you are sure they are happy with the product. Continue to pursue new customers through friends sharing with friends.

F. Enroll at least one customer out of every ten as a Marketer. Show them how they can build their own business through their contacts and these outstanding products.

Having studied the example of a Daily Action Plan above, now transfer the information from your worksheet section to the commitment page following. Make sure that the small reference numbers and letters match those from your worksheet on pages 35 and 36. Make copies and keep this "Action Plan Commitment" where you will see it often.

COMMITMENT TO AN ACTION PLAN
Yearly Goals

Date:_____, 199___

The **cause that drives me** to start my own Network Marketing business is:_____.

In 1 year I see myself living _____ with the freedom to_____ and with an income of $_____ as a result of my Network Marketing business. In order to attain my one year goal, I will achieve _____ level in the Company. I will notify the Company of my intent to pursue leadership level in the month of _____, 199____.

Creating Volume within my Organization

I COMMIT TO CREATING A WHOLESALE VOL-UME OF $_____ IN SALES EACH MONTH.

Of this volume, my family and I will personally use $_____. Therefore, I will retail the balance of this volume $_____ [A] for which I will be compensated $_____ in profits.

To achieve this, I commit to the following:

I will contact _____ [E] people per week about my product line.

Of those contacted, I will show the product to _____ [D] people per week.

Of those shown, I will establish at least _____ [C] new customers each week.

This will produce an average of _____ [B] customers each month.

Building Distributors in my Organization

I COMMIT TO ACHIEVING _____
LEVEL IN MY BUSINESS.

To achieve this level, in the first year, I commit to the following:

I will allocate ____ hours a day to my business.

Of this time, I will spend _____ hours per day (70% to 80% of my time) prospecting for new Networking Associates.

In order to generate _____ leaders on my front line:

I will create a total of _____ [1] who are willing to strive for this.

I will sponsor _____ [2] Network Marketers this year.

I will make a presentation or give information to _____ [3] people this year.

I will prospect a total of _____ [4] people in the first year.

This breaks down to contacting _____ [5] prospects per day with ___ day(s) off, to which I am totally committed. I understand this is the greatest challenge of my business.

To make contact with these ____ prospects daily/weekly, I will commit to the following plan:

(1) calling _____ people on my prospect list
(2) generating _____ leads through referrals
(3) contacting _____ people through lifestyling
(4) calling _____ from a client/organization list
(5) generating _____ leads through newspaper ads
(6) generating _____ leads by cold calling on business people
(7) generating _____ leads through speaking engagements
(8) generating _____ leads through business opportunity cards/flyers.

Part II

Power Multi-Level Marketing

Chapter 4

Methods of Recruiting

Our mentor Richard Kall repeatedly says, "The lifeblood of your Multi-Level Marketing organization is the new blood." What makes Richard so successful is his ability to recruit and support vast numbers of people.

As you study this all-out power approach—the equivalent of attacking Network Marketing with a wide open throttle—remember that *recruiting* is the key ingredient to success, after you have legitimate customers. In fact, it's usually easier to obtain retail customers by first showing them the business plan than it is to convert customers into successful recruiters.

Indeed, for those who approach MLM with limited goals, there is another way to recruit than the one we suggest here. That is to recruit only a few people, support them, and then go recruit more. We'll tackle that approach in *Part Three*. But if you want to be big time, a *power* Network Marketer, you must constantly recruit. This is a numbers game, and we're talking big numbers. It becomes a "people" business once new recruits demonstrate a desire to succeed, but you'll have to approach and recruit large numbers in order to find the winners.

This makes sense if you think about it. Even though Network Marketing is different in many ways from traditional business, all business is a numbers game. Every company that depends on a large sales organization pounds into the head of every salesperson that he or she must constantly seek new clients, if for no other reason than saturation and the assurance that there will always be a natural attrition of clients. Also, companies must have enough salespeople to cover the market with product.

In MLM you need as large an organization as possible to take up the slack for those who won't work or recruit, and to sell as much product as possible. Let's face facts: With the freedom offered by a Network Marketing organization, there is no way to make an individual do the work. It's all self-motivation, and no matter what amount of support and encouragement you give your people, you can't *force* them to do the work. The more people you have, the greater chance you have of getting real producers, of moving products, and of recruiting more producers into your frontline and downline. And finally—by the end of this book this will sound like a broken record—the foundation to success in the Network Distribution industry is word-of-mouth advertising. The best way to create a vast network of people talking about the products and company you represent is to recruit a host of people who will talk it up.

Establishing a Business Plan

As you get started and begin to establish your business plan, you will need to choose the recruiting methods that are the most appropriate for you to build your business. The following is a list in order of priority. As you go down the list, it generally takes a greater number to close.

Keep in mind as we discuss these recruiting methods that what we mean by width is your "frontline," the people you personally sponsor. You will tend to support these people more than the people below them. Depth refers to people brought in underneath the people you sponsored, or your "downline."

1: Build a prospect list.

This is not only the first but by far the most important way to begin by working through your center of influence. Fortunately, the ingredients for becoming successful using the list method are available to all adults who have normal social interaction. Social psychologists assert that the average person over the age of thirty knows more than *two thousand* people on a first name basis.

At first, this may sound outlandish to you. But we've found that if people sit down and seriously think through their centers of influence, beginning with elementary teachers, physicians, neighbors, then move to mechanics, salesclerks and on and on, they soon discover they know hundreds of people, some even thousands.

In this first phase make a list of those acquaintances, friends, and relatives with the purpose of calling on them in the near future.

To help trigger your memory, go to the library and get a book of vocations and avocations. Also get out a telephone directory and use it to recall names. Mark did just that when he began his MLM career with a small company in Utah. He was amazed at how quickly he came up with a list of 1,700 people he had known over the course of his lifetime. Rene worked from a memory jogger much like the one provided in her training manual, *The Encyclopedia of Network Marketing*. Do whatever it takes to make your list.

You must not impose limitations as you make your list. Do

not try to pre-qualify people you believe will or will not be interested in your MLM venture or who would be successful or unsuccessful at it. There are two reasons for this:

1. There's no way to gauge who will or will not be successful in Network Marketing. We have seen countless people who were corporate successes fail in Network Marketing quickly, while many, without any apparent qualifications, strike it rich in mere months.

2. *Too much analysis causes paralysis*. While making your list, realize you will end up never finishing it, or contacting the people on it, if you are busy trying to prejudge those you are listing. In traditional business, especially in the investment industry, sales managers try to motivate salespeople to action by convincing them that they have no business making a decision for clients before the client has had the opportunity to see the product. The same holds true for Network Marketing. Don't make your acquaintances' life decisions for them by not letting them see what you have to offer.

We suppose there will be a tendency for many of you to jump ahead and try to incorporate many of the eight phases of recruiting concurrently. Please don't. You simply will not have had enough experience yet, and this first phase of working with friends, family, and acquaintances is an important step in gaining both the experience and the working base you need to move on.

Do not move on to more difficult cold-calling phases until you are well on your way to making a list of at least 2,000 people and have worked with your warmer market. You should expect this process to take at least two to three months.

Let us address another problem that we have found common to newcomers in MLM. That is a reluctance to call on family and friends for the purpose of recruiting them into the business.

We understand the problem. Probably most of us have found ourselves in a situation similar to this: We were invited to an acquaintance's home for a dinner party. After dinner our host pulled out a blackboard and began drawing circles in an effort to get us into an MLM venture. We had no idea this was going to happen. We felt a little used, definitely like we had been invited under false pretenses. It left a bad taste in our mouths.

We have to tell you, however, that if you are one of those people who is reluctant to contact friends, relatives, neighbors, and acquaintances because you are afraid of leaving them with a bad taste or impression, then you are in the wrong business. We do have some suggestions, though, that might help you overcome your reluctance.

First, do not deceive people. That doesn't mean you have to tell them too much about the opportunity. But at least give them an idea of why you want to get together. Tell them you have a great money making opportunity. Or you might indicate you want their advice about a new venture. Or just say you want to discuss some business. We'll discuss approaches more in the next chapter. But remember, if you don't deceive people, you won't feel guilty when friends and family come to the presentation.

Also, know that you are really doing your friend or relative a favor. Remember that in recent years, a significant number of new millionaires came from this industry.

Considering that you have found an excellent Network Marketing business, you must believe that you are offering your friends and family a great opportunity for financial freedom and the time to enjoy that freedom. You must have the mindset that you are doing that person the greatest service of his or her life—rather than convey that you are approaching them to come help make *you* rich. Of course, they may not recognize it as a great opportunity and may even reject your proposal. However, denying your friends the opportunity to rise to great financial heights will create animosity once you have succeeded.

In our own downline, we have a man who just didn't believe he could approach his lawyer brother-in-law about his new Marketing venture. Within seven months this man was making six figures monthly. The brother-in-law was livid about not being given the opportunity to participate. The two still have not talked to each other.

If you succeed as a power Multi-Level Marketer, you are going to make vast sums of money. To do so you must make the list. If you are unwilling to make the list and contact the people on it, you are considering the wrong business.

2. Referral System

Reach out to people with whom your friends and acquaintances suggest you contact. Turn every *no* that you receive to joining you in this business into a possible referral. Do so by determining whether their decision not to participate is based upon lack of belief in this industry or the timing not being right for them. If it is the latter, you have the perfect opportunity to ask for a few referrals. Always be specific in your request: "*Who is the most well-connected person you know...the most fed up with the rat race of corporate life?*" And remember—if some of these people choose to enroll, the person who referred them may seriously reconsider joining your team.

If *you* are lacking in conviction or experiencing some self-doubt about your potential for success in this industry, you might consider using your list for the referral approach. Very simply, you approach some of the most well-connected, highly influential people on your list—those whom you are intimidated to ask directly to consider joining you in this business—and ask their help in getting your business started. Tell them that you are looking for highly motivated individuals who are fed up with the corporate world, who are concerned about security when they retire, or whose priority is to have more free time for their family. Be very specific as you ask for names. *"Who is that guy that everyone looks up to at your office? Wasn't your son-in-law expressing some disillusionment with his job the other night?"*

3. Lifestyling

When cold calling, make a concerted effort to seek people through the ordinary, everyday events of your life—what we call lifestyling. Go about your normal day (work, health club, bank, grocery store, day care, lunch with friends, seeing clients, working with customers, car repair, golf or tennis, etc.) and taking only seconds at a strategic moment, plant the seed about the business opportunity. You might say *"Have you ever thought about going into business for yourself?"* or *"With the kind of business you run, or with your communication skills, or with your contacts, you would be terrific at a business that I'm in. I'm not able to go into it now—I have to get on to my next appointment—but I would be happy to give you a call this evening, or leave this cassette for you to listen to while you're in your car."* Create a sense of urgency to be sure the audio is listened to as soon as possible. Make arrangements to talk further if the person finds this of interest.

4. Utilize clientele or organization lists

You may want to get mail lists to which you have access, e.g., former clients, teachers, real estate agents, sales organizations, clubs, alumni lists, small business owners etc. All mailings should be a provocative statement about time freedom and financial independence followed by a phone call. You may also call directly, breaking the ice with the fact that you are bonded as members of the same group. Then proceed to introduce them to the concept continuing to raise and not satisfy their curiosity.

Close by offering to mail or fax them some information, letting them know that, if the information you send interests them, you will arrange a meeting at your home for local contacts or by phone for those long distance.

5. Newspaper Ads

Newspaper advertisements will generally bring in a tidal wave of potential recruits. We know many of you will be tempted to use this phase first. Don't, no matter how great the temptation. If you jump ahead and try newspaper first, without going through the list phase, you may find you have little or no success with the ads.

Here's the reason. Look at the first few methods as your training period. Even though you may be uncomfortable buttonholing acquaintances, or those with whom you have even some remote association, once you do it, you will find yourself more comfortable with people you don't know. You have more latitude for mistakes with your friends. The three-to-five month phase of calling on persons on your list will give you knowledge and experience. It will cause you to learn answers to objections, so that you will be comfortable enough to do it with strangers. With the newspaper phase, you are going to need that experience.

Also, remember this: *The path to success in power Multi-Level Marketing is called duplication*—what is time tested and has worked for others. These things worked for us, and they are the sure steps that also worked for others. Why waste time and increase the odds against yourself by trying to reinvent the wheel?

This method involves placing ads for your business opportunity in your local newspaper. Be sure to stay within the guidelines and restrictions of local ordinances. Some countries do not permit newspaper ads. But where allowed, the ads are best used at specific times and in specific sections of the paper.

A shotgun approach usually results in wasted effort. Though we've heard of some success from people running ads in the sports section, we suggest you do not do this.

Here is what works:

Run the ad only on Sunday in the sales section of the want ads. This is the time of week when most people looking for sales jobs read want ads. All salespeople, or people who think they want to be salespeople, read the want ads and are looking for better opportunities. Or, run the ad everyday for three or four weeks.

There are two types of ads.

1. *The short ad*, designed for efficiency, to get the greatest response for the least amount of money.

Here is a good example of one that has proven very successful, but keep in mind this is only an example. Design your own.

100K FIRST YEAR
Commissions possible.
We need recruiters,
trainers, and managers.
Call (555) 555-1234

Of course, the bold headline of the potential income is the hook in this ad. There is good reason to state the potential income, while at the same time not giving specifics about the opportunity.

For under twenty dollars for a Sunday run, this ad generated *fifty* to *one hundred* leads a week every time we ran it.

2. *The long laundry list ad.* A long laundry list advertisement serves two purposes. First, it gives an impression of success in the person running the ad because that person obviously has the resources to run such an ad. Second, the ad presents an exciting opportunity because it uses several elements, or hooks bound to appeal on some personal level.

For example, the following is an ad that we have used several times—one which exemplifies the typical adult worker:

LET ME DESCRIBE YOU
- You have a nice home and decent car
- You are mortgaged to the max
- You find yourself stuck in traffic and smog
- You have all the plastic credit cards and you pay through the nose for them
- You're miserable with your job and life in general
- You may have marital problems and don't even know your own children
- You've had no significant vacation in the past five years
- And although you've won the rat race, you're still a rat

LET ME DESCRIBE ME
- At age 37, I'm semiretired, living in beautiful Aspen, Colorado
- After just one year, I'm making over $15,000 per month working only ten hours a week
- If I get tired of snow skiing and hang-gliding, I'll go to Barbados next month, or the next, whenever I feel like it
- I fly ultra-light aircraft, hang-glide, ski, and snorkel, things we all want to do, because I have the time and money to do it

For a personal interview call me at (555) 555-1234.

As you can see, it was a very long ad. It cost about $200 to run. But it achieved remarkable results. Within the first week, actually within the first two days after its appearance, we had 350 calls!

The key to writing and running the ads is that you must be creative. People like to read ads as long as they are *not* the typical "*we need help*" type.

Don't make ridiculous money claims or use your Company name in your ads. But neither should you be afraid to have fun writing your ads. Show your wild and crazy side. The purpose for this seeming insanity, besides trying to get a potential Distributor to read the ad, is to illustrate the playful, laid-back atmosphere of our organization that we hope will intrigue a recruit. Also, it helps to find people with a sense of humor. They help everyone work together.

You can come up with hundreds of different ideas. The ads can be long or short. But be creative enough to get the attention of readers. You do, and you will be inundated with potential recruits.

You may want to set yourself up with a local voice mail system to receive the calls. Put a provocative message on your system, one to two minutes, raising their curiosity and stimulating intrigue that will make the callers want to meet with you. Here is one such example:

"Congratulations on taking the first step toward your financial independence. We are currently looking for sharp, aggressive motivated people who are capable of building, training and managing a large national and international sales organization. (Refer to a recent publication concerning the success track record written about your company.)

If you are tired of making money for someone else and the 8 to 5 grind has lost its appeal, this may be the opportunity for you. And we provide complete training and support so that you will be successful!

You can work your business part-time, full time or big time; whichever method you choose to achieve the financial goals you have set for yourself. Don't worry. We are not looking for capital investors. The company is financially solvent. But we are looking for serious entrepreneurs who want to get in on the groundfloor of a new marketing trend. There is minimal investment and can be worked from your home. And we are in one of the most lucrative fields today (name the general category of your product).

If you would like to receive the facts about this exciting business just being introduced to your area, please leave your name, telephone number and fax number or address after the tone and one of our associates will contact you letting you know the material is being sent. If this interests you, then we can arrange to take this to the next step and set up an interview. We are looking forward to talking to you in the very near future."

6. Cold Calling on Business People

Cold calling is going out into the community and calling on successful people. Typically, they will be small business owners, managers, or corporate salespeople. For right now, forget about people who are out of work or who are failing in business. You won't have enough time to fool with them. Besides, you will find enough of those people on your list or through the newspaper ads. They will search you out, and some of them will become successful. But don't look for them when cold calling.

When embarking on the cold calling phase remember this: *You will be plagued by insurmountable opportunities.*

Why? Because if recent business magazines are anywhere close to being accurate in their assessment of the worldwide corporate predicament, at least *seventy-five* to *eighty percent* of all corporate workers hate their jobs and see them only as a way to survive. They get nothing more out of their jobs than a means to an end. Therefore, the vast majority of employees have a distorted view of what work is really supposed to be. Most would leap at any opportunity to depart the insanity of the rat race.

What does this mean for you, in addition to the obvious fact that almost the entire world of successful people are your candidates? How should this knowledge help your approach and attitude?

First, you need not fear rejection. Of course, some are going to reject you. But so what? Most are at least going to consider what you have to say. Next, it gives you an idea of how to approach most people.

Let's say that you are in an airport and you strike up a conversation with someone. Invariably, the question is raised as to what you do for a living. At that point simply say something like *"I sell financial freedom."* Now, keep in mind, that all you are doing is talking, making a friend. You don't necessarily have to say that line with a strong and imposing glare. People will turn off to you. You might, add something like, *"I'm in the business of helping people become financially independent by setting up their own home based distribution business. It's a whole new concept in marketing that is extremely lucrative."* At that point, the person is going to wonder what you are talking about. He or she will be interested, too, if just a little, because a person is a fool not to be interested in financial independence.

During this phase of recruiting, don't focus too much on products. Too many novice Network Marketers make that mistake, even though the products are important. They will come into play later. What interests the vast majority of people is financial independence and the time freedom that goes with it. At this point in their lives, most of the successful people you talk to have had numerous experiences with all sorts of product lines and gimmicks. What they want to know is how to achieve time and financial freedom.

That is why, when you are in a conversation with a potential recruit (that is, if you are on your way to becoming a power Marketer), you never indicate that the potential of the opportunity is $400 or $500 a month. Few people are interested enough in an extra car payment to take the time to pursue a new venture.

Instead, what you say to a stranger is, *"Would you be interested in an extra* $5,000 *to* $10,000 *a month?"* Or, *"If you knew for certain you could earn* $30,000 *to* 50,000 *a month and retire in three years, would that interest you?"* Almost everyone could use that kind of money. And you won't just be blowing smoke, because if they approach the venture the same way you are approaching it, then that kind of money, and more, is possible.

The salient issue is this: *Successful people want to know that there is unlimited potential in whatever they attempt.* You want recruits who don't believe there is a ceiling on their potential. So don't impose limits by suggesting a low earning potential. When you approach people about your Network Marketing venture, use significant figures. Remember the two greatest hooks are big money and free time. Never talk products in the approach.

There are myriad ways to meet new people during the cold calling phase. Go where you think successful people are conducting consumer business, or where they might hang out. Engage them in friendly conversation.

Check with the reference desk of your local library (or a nearby major library) for the *Businesswise or Crisscross,* which contains all businesses, broken down alphabetically by category, by zip code and by industry. If your library isn't familiar with this reference book by one of these names, describe what you are looking for. This gives the name of the owner/manager and if it is a large corporation, will list several hundred of the top V.P.s and department heads. Stockbrokers are especially familiar with this reference book. Choose according to what best suits you. Based on zip code, try to get within a five mile radius of your home, and concentrate on businesses with fewer than 10 employees. Since this gives names, you have the advantage of being able to ask for any individual by name.

You might also call on Mercedes, Olds, or Cadillac dealerships. Try banks, or savings and loans, or hotels where there are numerous business meetings everyday. Read business sections of the newspaper and see who is new in business, who's been promoted, demoted, or acknowledged. Call on local employment agencies and offer to show the owner or manager a way to permanently increase their bottom line. Regardless of which company their clients are placed with, those who choose to join them in this venture will be part of their organization forever.

An airport is a marvelous place. Successful people are always waiting, looking for a meaningful way to spend a few minutes (often hours). We have signed many people to our frontline whom we met for the first time in airports, some of whom have become very successful.

Often when opening the subject of Network Marketing to people you meet, you don't have to be particularly direct about it. One man in our organization has built his entire downline around what he calls a *third party referral* approach. When he meets someone new, he asks them, *"Do you know anyone who could use an extra five to ten thousand dollars per month?"* Of course, he isn't honestly looking for referrals, but he does get them. In the meantime, often the person to whom he is talking becomes interested and asks more questions about the venture.

Understand that you can be creative in your approach as long as you get out there, meet new people, and aren't deceptive about the venture itself. Sometimes you may just want to play with people and say something like *"Would you be willing to change brands of (deodorant, toothpaste, shampoo, select one of your most commonly used products) to make $10,000 a month?"* Just remember: the foundation of Network Marketing is word-of-mouth advertising. The best person to start that word-of-mouth is you.

Cold calling may be difficult for you at first, and the very thought of it may send cold shivers up your spine. But keep these points in mind.

1   By the time you have reached the cold calling phase, you will have spent several months performing easier recruiting methods. You will now have a good working knowledge of your business and better ways to answer questions and handle objections. That is why it is imperative not to cold call until you have performed the easier methods of recruiting your warmer market.

2.   You need not fear rejection. Though some will reject you, there are so many people who detest their current work and are open-minded enough to listen, that you will have all the new recruits you can handle without worrying about the people who reject the proposition outright. In all the years of cold calling, we've never had someone hit us or cuss us out. Rejection is a myth.

3.   Cold calling works. Put your effort into this method seriously for just a week, and you will have remarkable results.

7: Speaking Engagements

One of the most dreaded jobs in any organization—fraternal clubs, service organizations, professional associations, and corporations—is that of program director. The job of program director is usually temporary and normally lasts a year. The reason a program director's job is so dreaded is because that person is responsible for finding entertainment for the organization's meetings. That means finding a speaker, and good speakers are very hard to find.

That is your hole in the marketplace. There simply aren't enough speakers around. When you present yourself or your upline as a speaker you will find it easy to get speaking engagements.

If you haven't read Mark's book, *Power Speaking*, we encourage you to do so. He spent the past several years teaching power speaking across the country and several years prior on the speaking circuit to develop the concepts. In *Power Speaking*, you learn how to overcome the fear of public speaking, how to develop and deliver a moving presentation, and how to book engagements.

Public speaking establishes you on a high professional level in the Network Distribution industry. There is a phenomenon of automatic respect accorded to anyone who speaks in public. Also, though you won't get the number of recruits that the other methods yield, the recruits you do get will be extremely high-quality—people who are usually very serious about their inquiries.

One person on our frontline, who makes five figures monthly, has built her downline largely from her public speaking. Before her MLM venture, she had been the number one salesperson for a Fortune 500 company. Now, she delivers an after lunch speech for an association or service club every couple of weeks. She gives a very effective speech with some humor, a little more inspiration, but mostly her personal story of why she left a lucrative position in the mess called corporate America to enter Network Marketing. She touches on the Baby Boomers' social impact, rejection of the forty year plan, and concern for having security in their later years. Although the focal point of her talk is not about her company, she tells us that after every single speech, four or five people approach her with interest in her specific MLM venture.

Here's how you can accomplish the same thing. By this stage in building your organization, you will have been in Network Marketing close to a year. You will have met thousands of people and answered every conceivable question about your business and Network Marketing in general. You must realize that by now, you are an expert.

Develop a short twenty minute speech on the marketing trends of the '90s, how we've moved into the age of distribution, and why Network Marketing is the best distribution option. Get *Power Speaking* for help in writing and preparing the speech. Practice the speech many times. Then go to your city's Chamber of Commerce to get a list of clubs and organizations in your community. (Often corporations that regularly book speakers will also be included.) On the list you will find the names and telephone numbers of the program directors. Call them up and offer yourself as an after-dinner or lunch speaker as an expert on the marketing trends of the '90s. You will find it is quite easy to book engagements.

8. Business Opportunity Card Pass Out

This method can be extremely effective but must be used with discretion and good judgment. Make sure that you are complying with your company's policies and local ordinances. Write up something provocative on a business card not using the name of your company and, where permitted, pass it out appropriately (nice cars, airports, restaurant tables, fairs and convention centers, etc.). Or you might, in the course of conversation, say to someone: *"Do you enjoy what you do? Does it pay you what you're worth and give you enough time to do what you want?...I'm in the business of helping people build their own business. We're having unbelievable success in helping people create both personal & financial freedom. Here's my card. Call this number if you would like to set up an interview."*

Business opportunity cards work, but take a massive amount of handouts to be effective. The use of voice mail and answering machines can be useful. These cards are used as handouts, left in business places, your outgoing mail and bills and anyplace people can pick them up, put them in their pocket or purse and call later. Perhaps the most effective single source is placing them on cars. The best place to leave the cards is on the driver's door, above the door handle, inserted between the window glass and door felt. Do not place them under the windshield wipers since the card cannot be seen until inside the car and the driver may get irate by having to get out of the car to remove the card.

Following are some samples of cards that have proven to work effectively. The object of the card is to get people to call and leave their names and phone numbers. It is then up to you to call them back, get them some information and schedule an appointment.

Last year our top leaders earned more in a month than most corporate executives earn in a year!

If you feel you are above-average, that you deserve this kind of income and are willing to work harder than you've ever worked in your life, call:

(555) 555-1234

Either you want to retire with enough money and free time to feel secure and enjoy the best years of your life, or you don't.

Should You Quit Before You're Fired?

If the future of you and your job is uncertain ... if you are fed up with the rat race and the prospect of going back and forth for forty years, then consider this: There are legitimate alternatives to earning enough money and having the free time to feel secure and enjoy the best years of your life.

To learn more, call:

(555) 555-1234
24 HOUR RECORDED MESSAGE

Recruiting is absolutely essential to becoming a successful power Network Marketer. Even if you are entering MLM only on a part-time basis, you must know the essentials in case you later decide to make it your life's work.

Going wide, continually adding new people to your front-line, is the only certain way to become successful. This is because in MLM, more than in most businesses, there is a tremendously high attrition rate. The fact is you are going to have a lot of people quit because they are not willing to put forth the effort to do the things necessary to succeed.

Some so-called experts in MLM contend that the method of hiring a few people at first, supporting them until they become successful, then adding others is the road to success. But their approach will not succeed in the long term on a full-time basis. You cannot drag anyone across the finish line in *any* human endeavor, including Network Marketing. You will have people quit the venture, and it will break your heart because you have higher expectations for them than they have for themselves.

The only way to avoid unnecessary slowdowns from attrition is to continue adding to your frontline for at least two years.

Remember, as Richard Kall says, "The lifeblood of your MLM organization is the new blood."

These eight methods of recruiting—*the list, referrals, lifestyling, organizational memberships, newspaper ads, cold-calling, speaking engagements, and card pass-out*—are only the broad base for establishing a business plan for your recruiting efforts. You should perform them in the order that we give them because they form the path for your development and expertise in the business. However, they do not explain how to make a presentation to potential recruits and how to close the people joining your organization. That follows in the next two chapters.

We think a lot of people get their painful little shudder about MLM because of the deception often practiced on new recruits. How often we've been asked to a friendly little dinner party to discuss some business only to have a quick meal and then out comes a blackboard. As our host begins drawing circles we think, "Oh God, not this again." That is so unnecessary, yet we continually find people and companies that espouse it. We'll show you solid professional ways to present your business without deception.

Let's review:

- The lifeblood of an MLM organization is the new blood.

- Going wide refers to the frontline, the people you personally sponsor. Going deep refers to the downline, the people sponsored by your frontline, their frontline, etc.

- Continually going wide, increasing your frontline, is the best way to become a successful power Network Marketer.

- MLM is the only industry where, in one week, you can increase an organization from 10 to 250.

- There are eight methods of recruiting, from which you may select to establish a business plan:
  1. The list
  2. The referral system
  3. Lifestyling
  4. Clientele or organization lists
  5. Newspaper ads
  6. Speaking engagements
  7. Cold calling
  8. Card pass out

- Most people know at least two thousand people.

- Make a list of everyone you know. Use a list of occupations and avocations from the library to help trigger your memory. Remember the centers of influence in your life, such as schools, church, organizations.

- When making the list, do not overanalyze whom you think would be interested or capable. You cannot predetermine who will be successful. Too much analysis causes paralysis.

- Turn every *no* into a possible referral.

- Use your list for the referral approach if you are intimidated to approach certain individuals directly about taking a look at our business.

- Seek people out through the ordinary everyday events of your life—what we call lifestyling.

- Call on members of clubs and organizations using lists to which you have access.

- Do not move to the newspaper and cold calling methods until you have completed the list phase. You will need the expertise gained in the easy comfort zone of the warm market to accomplish the cold market phases.

- There are two types of ads: the short catchy ad and the long laundry list.

- Run ads only in the Sunday sales help wanted sections, or run ads daily in the classified sections of the paper for three or four weeks in a row.

- For long, laundry list ads, include enough elements to appeal to a wide cross-section of the population.

- Contrasts are a good way to design a long ad. Be funny or ludicrous. Be creative. The ad must stand out.

- A long ad gives the aura of a very successful venture.

- Expect positive results from cold calling because three quarters of workers detest their present jobs and professions.

- Try to approach corporate salespeople and owners of small businesses by using *Businesswise* or *Crisscross* from the reference desk of your local library.

- Go to high-priced auto dealerships, small businesses, hotels, airports and strike up conversations.

- Invariably, at least by the fourth question or topic of conversation, people ask what you do for a living. Say things like, "I sell financial freedom," to get their interest.

- When you mention money, use figures that are substantial. The people you are interested in do not want limits on their opportunities.

- Don't focus too much on products at this stage. Save the explanation of your products for the presentation.

- You need not fear rejection. There are plenty of people who detest their jobs and are open-minded enough to be interested in what you have to offer.

- To help you in public speaking, read a copy of *Power Speaking* by Mark Yarnell. It will help you prepare and deliver a moving speech.

- Book speaking engagements with clubs, corporations, and associations from a list from your local Chamber of Commerce. Booking engagements is easy because organizations have a hard time finding good speakers and the need is greater than the supply.

- Do not expect the vast numbers of recruits from speaking engagements that you will get from other phases. But typically, they will be high caliber individuals.

- Public speaking will enhance your professional standing.

- Create a general speech about the marketing trends of the '90s rather than on your specific opportunity. Practice it several times before delivering it. Keep speaking on a regular basis.

- Use Business Opportunity Card Pass-Out by leaving

cards with a provocative message in appropriate places (nice cars, airports, restaurant tables, fairs, conventions), or use them to exchange cards with someone you have just met.

• To become a power Multi-Level Marketer, you must continue to go wide for at least two years.

• You can't drag anyone across the finish line.

• Never be deceptive about your MLM venture. If you cannot be proud of what you do, then quit.

Chapter 5

Prospecting: The Initial Approach

Now that you know the basic recruiting methods and understand how to identify and come into contact with large numbers of people, you are faced with the problem of how to approach them.

Your single goal when approaching these people is this:

You must get them into your home for an interview and a well prepared presentation of your business opportunity.

Getting people into your home for a forty-five minute interview and presentation isn't particularly difficult when talking to people who have responded to your newspaper ads or to whom you spoke in a public speaking situation, though there are some peculiarities to those two phases we will discuss later. The tricky situations arise in steps one and six: the list phase and cold calling.

When discussing your business opportunity with acquaintances on your list or strangers in cold calling, you have only three means of contact:

1. The telephone
2. Face to face
3. Fax or computer

The first two aren't any great, eye-opening revelation and sound a bit simplistic. However, you must realize what you can and cannot accomplish using both means of contact, and how to use these approaches to your best advantage. The third is for a growing group of the more electronically inclined.

In using the telephone (the most efficient means of reaching the most people outside of ads), and in personal visits, you will make both *warm* calls(calls to friends and family from the list) and *cold* calls. But for both, there are two factors which are critical if you are to be successful in getting people to an interview.

- You must be credible and enthusiastic.

- You must always focus on potential financial rewards and free time.

Mentally prepare yourself to begin introducing your business opportunity to everyone. This is a crucial step in getting started and is often the make or break point of success. The more you exude strength, confidence, belief and enthusiasm, the more responsive people will be to you.

One of our favorite quotes is from the eminent theologian John Wesley who said, "If you catch on fire with enthusiasm, people will come from miles around to watch you burn."

That is particularly true in MLM. If you aren't excited about your networking opportunity, it will come across to those with whom you speak. What if you were the individual on the other end of the conversation and the person speaking to you down played what he was talking about? If he is so down on the program, why should you be interested?

Keep in mind that your objective is to get the prospect to attend your presentation (or pay attention to your multimedia package if long-distant)—not to tell them everything you know about your business at that moment. "Share the sizzle, not the steak." You can easily turn your prospects off by saying too much. If this is an area you find difficult, as many do, devote time to practicing it. Your personal demeanor, how you present yourself, is the very essence of Network Marketing. You cannot overdo the time you invest in your own personal development, so strengthen those qualities that will make you more credible.

Discussing large dollar figures plus free time as the upside potential is a method to excite the listener and pique his interest. In power Multi-Level Marketing, unless you are quite sure the person to whom you're speaking wants to be a part-timer, never use such small money inducements as $500 to $1,000 a month. Those figures just aren't going to intrigue most successful people, especially those who have been involved in sales for a long time.

The truth is, probably 90% of the people who become power Network Marketers do so because of the money. Therefore, you have to tell them the truth about the track record of successful Distributors making big dollars to entice them. At the same time you must use realistic figures. If you say the potential is easily $5,000, $10,000 or $20,000 a month, you are using meaningful numbers because that is far more than most people earn and is quite lucrative considering the additional benefits of freedom and being your own boss. Yet those figures are still well within the potential for earnings. If you use those numbers, you are not at all stretching the truth because the really heavy hitters in Network Marketing earn $100,000 to $200,000 per month and more.

When practicing inviting, mention only an exciting business opportunity and free time. You *must* avoid the temptation to discuss products until you make the presentation at your home. At that time, you will tell them all about the products and opportunity.

Approaching a Warm Lead

Let's discuss a way to approach a person on a warm call who is a friend or acquaintance.

You'll want to spend the first three minutes of the conversation with small talk, questions of health, wealth, or weather. Then go into the reason for your call.

"Jim, you're not going to believe what my wife and I have gotten into. We are more excited about this than anything we have seen in our entire adult lives and I want you to take a look at it. We are talking about more money in a month than most people make in a year and all the free time you've ever wanted!"

Avoid selling the Opportunity over the Telephone

At this point in the conversation, the person is likely to try and figure out what you are talking about. Is it a pet, an exercise program, a gold mine, or what? The temptation you will have is to start describing the program. It is important that you keep their curiosity piqued by saying as little as possible about the program.

This is not deception! We are not suggesting that you hide the fact that this is a business deal. In fact you should tell them that.

The point is, it is *impossible* to sell a person on participating in a business venture during a five to ten minute conversation over the phone. You are not selling a single product here, but trying to induce a friend to join you in a venture. There is no way for you to counter objections or explain all the intricacies without a solid presentation. All you want to do is get them to a presentation.

Early in our careers, as we were building our downline, we lost a lot of people from our list by telling them too much over the phone, thinking we could sell them on the opportunity in a ten minute call.

So, if a person asks you more about what you are talking about, that is when you should kick in more information about the financial potential. You can say something like:

"Listen, the opportunity is pretty intricate. I need to see you to go over the details, but I can show you how you can earn an extra five to ten thousand dollars per month. Let's get together on Wednesday."

Then don't say another word until the person responds. Assume the person is trying to see if he can meet with you on Wednesday. It is very important for you to suggest a time because it puts into his mind that you *will* meet with him. It turns the assumption away from *if* he will meet with you to *when*. If the person still tries to get more details, just assure him or her that it works. You might tell them a little about your upline's success and then be honest and say that it wouldn't be fair to him or you to try and discuss such an intricate but lucrative proposition on the phone. Assure the person that it is a business venture and then say "If Wednesday isn't good, let's shoot for Thursday." But whatever you do, pin them down on a day to meet at *your home*. And until you start making decent money, always use the income of someone in your upline as an illustration.

Remember, half will not show up unless you are very firm in getting them to commit to the meeting. None will show up if you tell them about the product or opportunity over the phone. Working through your entire warm market should take about two to four months.

When you have mastered your warm market approach, you will want to begin working in your cold market talking to ten, twenty, or thirty prospects each day—depending on whether you are doing this business slow time, part-time, or full -time.

The same rules apply to "cold" calls as well as "warm" calls. You must be enthusiastic, emphasize financial independence and free time, and get the person to a presentation in your home. There are some differences, however, in the style of your call. Presumably, the people you cold call don't know you from Adam. It would help if you could know a little about them, and you probably do, since you didn't just pick a name out of the phone book.

The way to approach a cold prospect, especially over the phone, is to first disarm your listener. The best way is to discuss challenges you might have had. Even if you haven't had any troubles, you probably got involved in a Network Marketing venture due to some dissatisfaction. One example of a successful approach for me is this:

"Jim, you know, just six months ago, my wife and I were suffering in this down economy. We were trying to figure out how we were going to make ends meet. Then a good friend of ours was kind enough to call us, just as we've called you today, and show us a new opportunity which has really changed our lives. Now I know, Jim, that you don't know me from Adam, but I'm so enthusiastic about this opportunity, and so convinced based on what little I know about you, that you could earn an extra five to ten thousand dollars a month or more. I really want to meet with you. Would next Tuesday or Thursday be better?"

Again, if the person asks for more information, avoid the details. State what facts you wish, like what you or your upline are earning or how many people are in your organization. If you don't have many, tell them how many people you hope to get. But stress that since it is a business venture they must come and see a presentation so they can get all the information and learn how to make big bucks. You must get them to your home for an interview. And never forget to suggest a time and then be quiet until they answer.

Never make a bad call!

We cannot overstress the fact that you must never, ever, make a bad call when trying to get a person to a presentation. That means if you do not feel enthusiastic, then don't make the call. If you don't have what you want to say ready, don't call. If you are going to stutter, hem and haw, say "uh" a lot, and if you lack confidence or at least don't believe you are prepared to sound confident, then don't make the call. You will do irreparable harm and lose a potential new Distributor if you do. If you can't make a good, enthusiastic call, don't make one.

Prepare yourself. Write down a few notes. Gather yourself beforehand. Pump yourself up. Think of objections and how you can counter them. We do that now in a minute or two. It might take you thirty minutes at first, but with practice, it will become second nature. If it takes thirty minutes, an hour, whatever, take the time to be prepared mentally before you call.

Fighting the Fear of Rejection

When making warm or cold calls, one thing that will work against you, the one thing that has a tendency to dampen your enthusiasm, is the fear of rejection.

One trick we use that helps us overcome the rejection-fear and the potential of dampened spirits is to realize that each call is money in the bank—even if they say *no*.

Our experience has been that we'll get about one positive response on cold calls for every ten we get on warm calls. But that one, more often than not, joins our organization. One person who really attacks Network Marketing in a power way might earn us $10,000 a month. It's not uncommon for cold contacts to earn us at least $1,000 a month. Thus, every call we make results in money whether that person becomes involved or not.

Notes on the Face to Face Prospecting

We haven't mentioned much about face to face prospecting because the same rules for telephone calls apply to personal calls: Be enthusiastic, talk big dollars, prepare before you go— even if it's to a party—and don't disclose too much information. Your goal is to get people into your home, on your turf, for a presentation on the MLM opportunity.

There are a few peculiarities about face to face prospecting that should be mentioned, however.

In terms of numbers, you cannot meet as many people in person as you can by phone. However, it is a lot more difficult for people to tell you *no* to your face. That is just human nature. So while you can't see as many people, the percentage of people who will accept your invitation will be much higher.

Also, you and the person to whom you are speaking, whether "warm" or "cold," will have a tendency to want to speak in detail about your opportunity right then and there. You know what we're talking about—the old "cocktail napkin" presentation. Don't you suggest it. If the person to whom you're speaking suggests it, laugh it off. There is nothing professional about a cocktail napkin presentation. You can't possibly remember all the details, and you are at a disadvantage by not being on your own turf. Just talk about big money and free time and try to set a home appointment date.

The best approach, after breaking the ice with small talk, is something like this:

"I'd like to ask you a crazy question, but I'd appreciate a serious answer. If you knew for sure that you could double or triple your present income and enjoy complete time freedom at that income level, would that interest you?"

Those who answer *yes* are prospects. Simply request their card and tell them you will be calling them for an interview. No matter how persistent they may be in requesting additional information, don't give it. Just get their card and explain that you are in a hurry to get to your next appointment.

Approaching People Who Respond to Ads or Speeches

Even though you won't know the people who respond to ads or meet you after a public speaking engagement, you can consider all those people "hot" prospects in that they are coming to you for information about the opportunity.

However, just as in the list and cold call methods of recruiting, your goal is to get them to an interview in your home, or in a hotel suite or meeting room if you are out of town.

You might try suggesting in your newspaper ads that you will not discuss the opportunity over the telephone, but that they should call you to set up an appointment.

As a rule, you will get many calls from your ads, and you won't have so many contacts from speaking, though the ones you do make will be very interested. When people call or talk to you, you must still be very enthusiastic and stress financial rewards and time freedom. Still, suggest a time to meet, though you might also add that you will be having a group presentation at a particular time. This will increase the evidence of widespread interest.

If you recall the short ad in the previous chapter, you have one other factor to use to induce people to a presentation. That is, we stressed in the ad that we are looking for trainers and managers. As we pointed out, most of the people who call on the ads will be experienced salespeople, who always look at the Sunday ads for good opportunities. Those people may be tired of *just* selling and would like to manage people or train them. Stress the management aspect of the opportunity when responding to people who call on ads, and you will get a much larger acceptance to your invitation to meet in your home.

Using Fax or Computer

There is a growing number of people who have and use facsimile machines and/or computers. It is the age of technology and don't be afraid to use it if you have access to it. Fax machines link us to our next door neighbor as readily as to a trans-Atlantic acquaintance on the other side of the world.

There are two ways to use fax machines: (1) by actively sending a letter and information to a targeted audience, or (2) setting up a fax-on-demand and giving out the phone number to anyone interested in knowing more about your exciting business.

With the introduction of the super-information highway, the use of computers for national and international recruiting purposes has never been easier. Millions of people are joining Internet services. There are many of them and the number grows daily. Currently the most popular interactive services reported to us to get you online are America On-Line (the easiest to use), CompuServe (the least expensive), and Prodigy (the most users). You will need to check current standings (trial memberships are a good way to do this) and see which service fits your needs best. Simply place a provocative ad, much like you would a newspaper ad, in the appropriate category on your online service, e.g., under "entrepreneur" and then under "sales position" or the like. As online services grow, even better methods of marketing will develop. Once you have had a response to your ad, *e-mail* allows you to communicate with anyone in the world relatively inexpensively. It is clearly an interesting way to reach out to online users and build an international network of Marketers in your organization.

Take some time to browse the net for MLM-related topics, and be sure to check out the Yarnell web page which includes up-to-date information on recruiting, training and accessing our training materials.

Pre-Market Activity

Some of you will be privileged to join companies which grow and prosper in your primary country, then expand globally. Thus, you need to understand the fundamentals of pre-launch recruiting. We have built dynasties in foreign countries by following procedures which anyone can follow. First and foremost, *do not* attempt to distribute any products in advance of your company's official opening date as that may jeopardize your entire company. Remember, until all product ingredients have been approved by a new government, your products are illegal. Additionally, *do not* sign up new Distributors in any new country until your company's official launch date as that could also jeopardize future business. And finally, *do not* bring citizens of another country into your own to sign them up in advance of official expansion because signing them up early is against most company policies, is not duplicable, nor is it fair to the other Distributors in your country who cannot afford that process. Having said those things, here's the key.

You want to build a pre-launch "verbal network" of committed future Distributors. Select one or two front line people who have major connections in the country about to open and teach them to contact their top 100 friends. Each of those people are then asked to make the verbal commitment to become involved in the business at the time the company officially opens. Of those 100, some will get particularly excited about the business. It is those prospects whom you then train to also begin a verbal network.

They will be shown how to begin meeting in small groups in their homes to introduce the industry to people not yet familiar with it—the timing, the trends, and how money is made through exponential growth and leveraging. They want to then name the company they have chosen, describe it's history, fiscal stability, and product line. They might conclude by describing why they are joining this company and a particular organization within it—describing their strengths and advantages.

The key is to build a committed network of future Distributors so that when the company opens you will have an immediate downline. To those who show moderate interest, you might say: *"You'll be hearing more about this company, and if you should decide later on that you would like to take a look at it, I hope you'll give me the first chance to show you what it is all about."* All of this can be done without actually violating any policies and procedures and you'll end up with an advance network without in any way jeopardizing the future opportunity for others.

Handling Initial Objections

When setting your appointments, whether in the warm or cold market, be prepared for the inevitable question, "What is it?" You might prepare a response something like this:

"It is a brand new division of a ___ year old company that has recently expanded here. The parent company has hit _____ dollars in sales and they are looking for assertive people like you who can conceive of making huge incomes. Don't worry! They're not looking for capital investors. The company is fiscally solvent. But they are looking for serious entrepreneurs who want to get in on the groundfloor. (I thought of you right away.) That's why I want to get together with you. Now you know how to get to the corner of (continue without pause to give directions to your home)."

If they persist in asking questions, close it off by saying:

"If there were a way that I could explain all of this to you in a few minutes on the phone, I would. But there is no way that I can do justice to it. It is a visual concept that you need to see for yourself so that you can decide if it's right for you. I can only promise you that getting together to check this out will not be a waste of your time. Now you know how to get to the corner of..."

If you're not getting the help you do need from your sponsor, go up the line until you find someone with whom you are comfortable. You begin by making appointments for private presentations or, if they are long-distance, by sending out audios or videos on the business opportunity. It might be difficult at first to contact your ten to twenty best people, but learn to work above your comfort zone. Remember, you are doing them a favor—not the other way around. You have something people can't get anywhere else. If *you* don't introduce them to your products and the opportunity, someone *else* will.

Let's review:

- Your goal on the initial approach in recruiting is to get people into your home for a presentation of your business opportunity.

- The three means of contacting people are by telephone, face to face, and by fax or computer. You reach the most people through telephones, but it is more difficult for people to say *no* in person.

- When making the contact, always be enthusiastic and focus on large financial rewards and free time.

- Never try to sell the MLM opportunity on initial contact. You are selling a new business venture, not a product.

- It is impossible to sell a business opportunity over the phone. If you try, you could lose the prospective Distributor to your organization forever.

- When cold calling, disarm the listener with truth about the impact the opportunity has had on your life.

- Always suggest a specific time when you and the person to whom you are speaking can get together. Get a commitment.

- Never make a bad call, by phone or in person. Prepare yourself. Write notes about what you want to say. If you are not feeling enthusiastic, don't make the call.

- Overcome the rejection-fear by realizing that every call is money in the bank—even if they say *no*.

- The best face to face approach is to ask a leading question, get their number and permission to follow up with a call.

- Don't yield to the temptation and attempt an on-the-spot presentation at a personal meeting. No "cocktail napkin" presentations. They aren't professional.

- With people who respond to your ads, refuse to discuss the opportunity over the phone. At speaking engagements, don't discuss details after the meeting. Make appointments for your home instead.

- An additional inducement to people who respond to ads is management and training opportunities.

- Fax machines link us to our next door neighbor as readily as to a trans-Atlantic acquaintance. Use them to quickly communicate facts about your business.

- If accessible, use a computer online service to prospect and *e mail* to communicate afterwards, especially for national and international prospecting.

- When expanding into a new foreign market, you may want to begin building a *verbal network* of committed future Distributors, and teach those most excited to do the same.

- Be prepared to handle initial objections like "What is it?" Have a strong prepared response to this and any other objection designed to avoid appointments.

Chapter 6

The Opening Interview and Presentation

The first interview should be held in a personal setting and is the most important part of building an enormous downline necessary for success in power Multi-Level Marketing. It is the follow-through in recruiting. We suggest it be held in your home, your living room perhaps, and not in someone else's office, a motel room, or in a bar using cocktail napkins.

Your presentation should consist of eight steps. All these steps fit together like links in a chain and you should not omit any of them. The eight steps are:

1. Introduction: Your story
2. Credibility phase: Your company and its products
3. Trends: Causes of MLM momentum
4. Shock phase: Money and free time
5. Media phase: Show a video
6. Board demo: Your compensation plan & leveraging
7. Q & A: Stress your support and proven system
8. Closing: Reasons to get involved

Let's explore these eight steps in detail.

Step 1: The Introduction

Your goal in the introduction is to prepare people for the rest of the interview. You are creating an atmosphere of importance and professionalism for the listeners about the Network Marketing opportunity. Before beginning, hand out something for them to read—an article about your company or a corporate brochure—something about the business opportunity and not merely about your product.

Open the meeting by explaining the background and circumstances of your life, showing perhaps how you were on a one-way collision course with poverty before discovering this opportunity. Tell them of the reservations and skepticism you had when first seeing this. Talk about your life at the point you discovered Network Marketing: climbing the corporate ladder, going nowhere, stress, no time for family; or owning your own business, slave to the job, cash flow problems, payroll headaches. This is a good time to talk about your values—those things that matter most to you, like your family and accomplishments you hope to acheive once you have been successful in this business.

Share the fears you experienced about making the transition and how your family or friends downplayed Multi-Level Marketing. Explain your own skepticism. Talk about the people to whom you spoke to check out this company and how, when you could find no downside, you joined. Share your goals, what you have accomplished or are working toward. If you are still in the process of achieving your goals, conclude with a success story of someone in your upline or company who is your mentor.

We know this is simple enough, but there is sound psychology behind the personal story approach, and it is extremely important in your follow-through as you progress with the presentation. If you will recall, in earlier chapters we pointed out that the only way to sell your opportunity to others is with enthusiasm. Rather than trying to spout accolades about a company or plan, or attempting to extol hypothetical virtues, the best way to demonstrate enthusiasm is to tell people what the opportunity has meant to you personally. People love anecdotes and personal stories. They can relate to them. *Through you they will see tangible results of the benefits of the program.*

As in all parts of the first presentation, this step must be well thought out and prepared ahead of time. It wouldn't hurt for you to practice it. Never speak off-the-cuff or try to come up with impromptu witticisms during this step. Even if you think you are good at it, you probably aren't nearly so good as you suppose, and the impromptu statements will probably lead you off the path.

Another reason for solid preparation is that this step should be brief. *The entire presentation ideally lasts only forty-five to sixty minutes.* You can not linger at this point. If you are not well prepared, you could take valuable time away from necessary steps later.

Here are a couple of ideas you might use to guide you in preparing your introduction:

- Tell candidates a little about your personal and financial situation. Tell them how, at the time you joined your Network Marketing company, you and your family sought to get out of financial pressures, away from stress, off the forty year plan, and ultimately, you felt a need to create a plan for long-term passive residual income.

- Whatever your reasons for getting into Network Marketing, don't be afraid to tell potential Distributors. More than likely, most of them either will be in similar circumstances or at least will identify with some of your sentiments.

- Tell why you believe Network Distribution is more viable than traditional business. It won't hurt to let candidates know a little of your personal philosophy, and it just might help them put into words some personal feelings they've been trying to express.

Step 2: The Credibility Phase

The purpose of this step is to provide credible information that the company is a growing and accepted firm and presents a viable opportunity for the potential candidate. You must show that what you are presenting represents something real.

In this information age, the way to do that is to give your prospects any magazine articles, newspaper stories, and testimonials of happy customers of your company and its products. If these were passed out at the beginning, refer to them now.

You should seriously question joining or remaining with any MLM firm which doesn't already have some positive magazine or newspaper article written about it. If a company doesn't have such stories, it more than likely is too small or too young. Also, if there aren't already a large number of satisfied customers by the time you are getting in, then it is either a bad company or too young for you to know whether or not it even has a chance for success.

As with the introduction, this credibility phase should last no more than five minutes. Recruits don't need to read every word of every article, not yet anyway. At this point, knowing they exist is enough. Highlight the salient points and make sure you have enough copies for everyone.

Step 3: Trends

Timing is everything! The largest and strongest demographic trend of this century has changed the face of business as we know it. It's called the "Baby Boomers." They are 90 million strong, born after World War II between 1946 and 1964, and represent one-third of the North American population.

The trends pervading our society have much to do with the momentum being experienced in our industry. Most people are fed up with the forty year plan offered by traditional business. They are sick of going back and forth to work, back and forth like a silly, caged lion. They are tired of bosses, meaningless memos, unreasonable quotas, and expending all of their energy making someone else wealthy. The boomers have seen this plan fail their parents and grandparents, and are not willing to gamble all their hopes and dreams on a gold watch and a pension program that results in most people living well below their standard of living at near poverty level.

Security is the cornerstone not only of the American Dream, but of people's dreams worldwide. However, there is no security any more in traditional business or government. Most Baby Boomers realize that it takes two incomes to achieve an average standard of living, and there have been too many layoffs by too many solid companies for anyone to believe their future is secure just because they have a job. Many people today not only want out of the rat race, but more importantly they want to create residual income that can be counted on into the retirement years.

The Baby Boomers make the government subsidized retirement program possible. Like a giant Ponzi scheme, 76 million Baby Boomers feed into the Social Security stream in the US. Therefore many older people today have some degree of security, pittance that it is, because of the upstream flow being generated. But what happens when these Baby Boomers move downstream and become the *recipients* of Social Security, with a much smaller segment of society feeding the stream? What happens when people are living longer using up more of the funds? More and more people are realizing that government subsidized programs are a myth for the Boomer and fringe Boomer generations and are realizing that they can't count on being subsidized in their retirement years. It is critical that they begin taking charge of their lives and making some responsible plans for creating residual income for their later years.

Baby Boomers are trend setters. When they were babies, they turned the diaper industry into a multi-billion dollar business. As they got old enough to scrape their knees, they made Dr. Spock a household word. When they became teenagers, they turned a little store called "The Gap" and fast food stores like "McDonalds" into major franchises. When the oldest of the Boomers reached their 30's and began experiencing their first bulges and sags, they made Jane Fonda exercise videos and health club memberships go off the charts in sales. Now moving into their 40's and 50's, the Boomers don't want to show any of the signs of aging. The Baby Boomers are spending literally billions to create a quality extended life on Retin-A, organically grown food, health club memberships, workout tapes, exercise equipment, cosmetic surgery, and all kinds of nutritional and personal care products that help them have longer, healthier quality lives.

Remember that these Boomers stand to inherit trillions of dollars in the next two decades! This is the only time in history when all 18 years of the Baby Boomers will be participating in one trend at one time.

Incredibly, the *international* market looks even more promising. The European Common Market represents another major market to be captured and the business potential in the Pacific

Rim is greater than in the US and Europe combined! Over 1.8 billion people live in the Pacific Rim. In just a few years 30% of those people will be in their 30's and 40's. That's almost 600 million people creating another business explosion and age wave of staggering proportions. It's going to be 10 times larger than the one we're experiencing in the U.S.!

Companies carrying superior personal care, nutritional and fitness products are in the marketplace ready to respond to the Baby Boomer obsession, and with products of high enough quality to satisfy even the affluent segments of the population. All the right forces have combined to create an explosive situation.

Network Marketing has come of age and is the true trend of the future. The Baby Boomers are driving it because they don't want to end up like their parents and grandparents, the generation who got duped by the promises of the 40 year plan. They want both personal and financial freedom. The Boomers and fringe Boomers are also driven by an insatiable desire for living longer, healthier lives. Therefore, the combination of these two phenomena are propelling personal care along with the health and fitness business into explosive growth. In 1994, just among U.S.-based companies, sales in household and personal care alone exceeded $68 billion, and that figure is expected to be substantially larger by the end of the decade. It is also projected that over this next decade, as much as half of everything sold will be sold by word of mouth through Network Marketing. Can you imagine what will happen to these statistics when considered on a worldwide scale?

To substantiate this fact, *McLean Magazine* reported that 1991 was the worst year for advertising since the end of World War II. 23% of department store sales are being rung up by stores in bankruptcy. U.S. Sprint and MCI are now using Network Marketing, and have just had the greatest growth spurt in their histories. It is also being used by AT&T, General Motors, Gillette, Mastercard and the list goes on. Fortune 500 companies are just learning what the Network Marketing industry has known for over 40 years: Network Marketing offers the only effective means to bring top-quality merchandise to consumers at a reasonable cost. And this awareness is gradually being carried into every major country.

Step 4: The Shock Phase

We *used* to advocate during this step, showing the huge paychecks of super successful people in your upline or from your company. The purpose was to shock people, especially those who had been successful in other industries, into understanding and visualizing the huge potential rewards of your MLM opportunity.

Now we no longer do this. One reason is because many state attorneys general, always vigilantly scrutinizing our industry, view showing the large checks of heavy hitters as a means of misrepresenting the true earnings of the majority of individuals inside MLM organizations and as a way of misleading people.

If you don't mention the hard work involved in attaining a power Marketer's income level, if you try to use a full-timer's check to recruit part-timers, if you fail to mention the huge numbers of people who never take off in this industry, or if you fail to focus on the products your company sells, then indeed you are misleading and misrepresenting the facts. Unfortunately, some Marketers don't mention those things in their presentations and just focus on the huge potential rewards. By so doing, they fail to approach their presentations with integrity and thus hurt us all. Do notice, however, that we focus on those aspects of the business in other parts of this book.

How do we put the shock in the shock phase? You must still mention the huge potential rewards. To not do so would also be misleading. You can still explain that the sky is the limit as long as you point out that if you don't duplicate the program, then the sky isn't so bright. Stress the huge potential rewards strongly and accurately. Talk up the homes, cars, boats, and trips you or those above you enjoy. Stress the possibility of financial freedom and the time to enjoy it. Share the philanthropic opportunities for those who have goals bigger than themselves. Make this part of the presentation strong. Show what happens when the recruit joins the program if he duplicates it. Then show the downside of not doing the work.

Another thing you can do is tell the story of a real person you know, of the struggle they've had in traditional business. You might contrast that with a story of success of someone in Network Marketing. One thing we do sometimes is discuss the number of people, who at age 65, after staying on the forty-year plan treadmill, must still rely on their children or the government to survive. According to the most recent statistical poll we've seen reported, out of every 100 people who reach the age of 65, 31 are dead, 68 are living well below their previous standard of living, and only 1 is wealthy. And among those who achieve wealth, they have often paid for it with stress-induced coronaries or cancer. We all know people in that predicament. Build a story around this because, be assured, people don't want to be destitute or rely on their children in their old age. Also remember, someone somewhere in your upline is earning big money. Tell their story. If your company releases income averages, share that information. The shock phase should always include these type of examples as well as a discussion of a $30,000 to $50,000 a month upside potential of our industry. This is reasonable since many top leaders make far more than this.

Step 5: The Media Phase

All you do during this step is to show a video tape or play an audio cassette which explains your particular MLM opportunity, the company, its products and compensation plan, and any other pertinent information.

We strongly suggest that you use a video presentation if at all possible. Most companies have video tapes available. If the company you are with has neither video nor audio tapes available directly, or individuals in the upline don't offer them, then again you must reconsider your association with them.

Search out videos from people in the upline. They are often more compelling as a recruiting tool than materials produced by the company. Finally, no matter how many times you have seen the presentation and no matter how bored you might get with it, never leave the room. Stay there during the entire tape.

By staying in the room, you deter potential recruits from visiting with each other and it will keep their minds on the taped presentation. Also, if you leave the room, there is always a wise guy who disrupts things by making what he thinks is some neat witticism, usually a negative remark about the tape. So, discourage talking to focus attention on the tape and keep the interview moving.

Step 6: The Board Demonstration

For the board demonstration you stand up, use chalk on a chalk board, or erasable marker on a white board to show these two points of the MLM opportunity:

1. Your company's compensation plan.

2. An example of how exponential growth in MLM works to an individual's benefit.

The first part of the demonstration is an uncomplicated explanation of the company's payment plan and its requirements. We can't tell you what those are because each company is different. For example our company pays up to fourteen percent on each level below us, until a person below reaches executive status. Then it pays five percent, six levels deep. You will have to explain what levels and percentages your company pays, what it takes to reach executive or supervisor status and so on.

Most people will forget seventy-five percent of the details once they walk out of your living room. Bring out the salient facts and avoid minute detail. For example, you must explain and illustrate how a person can get to the maximum pay-out offered by your company. Be sure to memorize all these facts and information and how you intend to present them well in advance. You must appear knowledgeable and cannot waste time trying to figure out where you are going and what you want to say.

Perhaps the more important part of your board demonstration is the example of how exponential growth occurs and how individuals can make the fabulous incomes you've mentioned. It is almost as important as the "shock" phase. It shows how leverage works: the benefits of thousands of people in a downline and how rapidly that downline can grow.

The five by five example

The example we use is what we call the "five by five" example. We write on the board:

$$5 \times 5 \times 5 \times 5 \times 5$$

We explain that the purpose of this illustration is to show how dramatic exponential growth can become in a matter of just five months using a factor of five. In other words, if the recruit signs up only five people in the first month, trains those five to do what he did so that they each sign up five the following month, and then those do the same, that person has phenomenal growth in his downline.

In the first month there are five; the second, 25; the third, 125; the fourth, 625; and the fifth, 3,125. Add them together and by the end of the fifth month, with just five people adding five people every month, a person has almost 4,000 people in the downline.

So we write down—4,000—on the board. But we don't leave it at that. Because it isn't really the truth and everybody with any sense knows it. We point out that attrition is a very significant factor in MLM as it is in all business. We explain that they can't really expect to retain all 4,000 people. In fact, in order to be conservative we explain that they must assume they will lose as many as 75 percent of their people who will either give up or fail to duplicate the system properly. We then draw a line through the 4,000 and write 1,000 below it. Now that is realistic.

But don't stop there with your scenario of low-balling the numbers, because you want to illustrate that even with only moderate success, a person can make it big. So we suggest that they now assume that each of the remaining 1,000 are only selling or using $100 in products each month. That isn't very much, but you have to assume that some of the people in the downline aren't working very hard while only a few are really moving product through their organization. However, and this is the point to drive home, 1,000 people moving or using just $100 in products is $100,000 in group volume.

What does that mean? If your company pays a 10% override once you have achieved executive or director level, you would be earning $10,000 a month at this stage. In our company, we explain, it means that in the fifth month, with our fourteen percent override, we would get a check for $14,000!

Think of the impact of this example, of the power of being

realistic rather than blowing the numbers out of proportion. You've made the recruit see that—by recruiting just five people and no more, after losing three-quarters of his downline, and by having only modest individual sales—he can still earn a substantial figure a month by the fifth month. Mark started the same way and after his fourth month actually earned more than $14,000.

Here's an important point to remember. Some people in the Network Distribution industry would have you believe that you are better off appealing to people who want to earn an extra five or six hundred dollars a month and that you should avoid the big figures because they scare off some people.

They do have a point. You certainly do not want to discourage part-timers, and yet you want to give them something to reach for as well. If you know you are addressing people who are more part time, product oriented, you might suggest that they join your company with the modest goal of redirecting their spending to use $100 a month of product they are already using anyway: *"Just suppose that you commit to this plan of using $100 per month of product you are already using. You redirect your spending to a higher quality product line, and every month you commit to finding just one other person willing to do the same; that is redirect $100 a month of their spending to higher quality product they are already using, and find one person willing to do the same. At first your volume grows slowly—$200, $400, $800, $1600, $3200, $6200, etc. But with the power of exponential growth, if everyone were to consistently duplicate this simple program, at the end of 14 months, you would have created an organization volume of over $1.6 million of product orders per month, of which, in our compensation plan, you receive 5%, or a check of over $80,000 per month. That puts your annual income at about one million dollars per year. We call this the 'Millionaires Club.'"*

We have a Distributor in our organization named Kei Itaka who actually did this. After just 14 months, he created an organization of over 30,000 people of which 16,000 were purchasing a monthly average equivalent to $100 a month of wholesale product. Obviously, this is not easy to achieve or duplicate. Someone is likely to break the cycle, meaning that it will take you longer or you may not reach the full goal. But ask yourself these questions: *Do you have a better plan for achieving financial and time freedom? What if it takes you two or three or even four times as long? What if you only reach half way? Or a quarter of the way? Or a tenth of the way? Could you be satisfied with just $100,000 a year of residual income?*

In both examples of leveraging, you have given people a vision of what is possible, although you are clear that this is not likely to happen easily. While you don't want to exaggerate or overstate the possibilities, you do want to carry the explanation of the opportunity to the maximum extreme so that you can intrigue people who are already successful. You will never recruit bank presidents and CEO's of major corporations nor will you attract national sales managers if they think that they can earn only $600 or even $4,000 a month. Always show you prospects the big picture. That's what excites people.

Step 7: Questions and Answers

Now is a good time to take questions about the preceding information. Answer all the questions that relate to the presentation, keeping in mind that if anyone leaves with major questions, chances are he or she will not sign up with your organization. On the other hand, don't become too technical in your answers.

Also, avoid negative questions about the program. By negative, we mean distracting questions like how many of the total organization really make those big bucks. Just say that the big bucks are there for anybody who follows the plan. Don't let skepticism rule the session either. Just answer politely and say that if the skeptic isn't satisfied by the end of the presentation, you'll talk about it then. Whatever you do, don't dwell on negatives or let negative people influence your recruits! Be strong. Retain total control of the interview.

Keep your focus on making certain that the little knowledge they retain when they walk away is the correct information. Let your answers always bring them back to seeing the long range potential of big money and free time.

Take this time to stress the support and proven track record of success that are available in your organization. Tell them about the accomplishments of those in your upline and of the system that so many have used to make it to the top. You want them to know that if they join your organization and follow this system without reinventing the wheel, that they too have the chance to create the lifestyle of their dreams.

Step 8: Closing Comments

Point out that it doesn't make sense *not* to become a Distributor in your company:

1. You have the opportunity to purchase, at cost, the finest state-of-the-art products on the market today, saving yourself the retail markup you now pay at a store for inferior products.

2. If you are in the employ of someone else, you have no tax deductions. Becoming a Distributor in your company can give you all the tax benefits of owning your own business, including travel and inheritance. What you build can be passed on to your own children and your children's children.

3. If you are on the forty year plan and want off, if you want to take charge of your life, you have the opportu-

nity to build your own business with unlimited potential and ongoing income. This is the greatest opportunity in the history of free enterprise.

We have: the right corporate team
the right products
the right trends
the right compensation plan
the right kind of leverage
the right support

Remember. There are two types of people in this world: those who think they can and those who think they can't. And they're both right! The choice is up to you.

During this step, in addition to what you gave them when they first came in, hand out something for recruits to take home and read or hear.

If no one in the company has created an audio cassette that explains the business, then you create one for recruits to take home. It is extremely necessary to help the recruit handle all the negativism and objections he is going to encounter in his own mind and from others who weren't there with him.

Remember: The most critical hours in a potential new Distributor's life with your organization are the twenty-four hours after the first presentation. No matter how excited the candidate might be when he or she leaves your presentation, they will have a difficult time confronting the skepticism of spouses and friends who were not there to hear your presentation. You cannot imagine how many high caliber people have left our living room all pumped up only to call in a couple of days to say their spouses wouldn't *let* them join.

We find it difficult in this day and age to believe that a spouse could get away with forbidding their husband or wife to do anything. But any spouse can create a lot of negativism which keeps new recruits out of the business.

However, if that new recruit is armed with an audio tape that provides good and valuable information—something a recruit could use after saying to a spouse, "*Don't believe me, listen to him,*"—then you will have helped ward off negativity from spouses and other primary objections that surface in the first twenty-four hours.

Close by inviting them to the next regularly scheduled training meeting. Never allow them to leave without a new date to return to your home or office.

An Optional Step: Forbidden Fruit

Let's go back to the first step, the introduction where we said you must tell why you got into Network Marketing. During this step we add a part which some of our associates question but we have found valuable. It's all up to you.

To take all the pressure off the potential recruits, we say, "*We wouldn't sign you up today even if you begged us. In fact, if you don't go home tonight and lose sleep just thinking about this opportunity, you're not a good candidate.*" We have two reasons for doing this at the beginning.

The first is that we want to make it appear that we're taking away the opportunity before we even give it to them, just for psychological reasons. You know, to create forbidden fruit. We also don't want them to feel they are under pressure to be signed up that day. One of our organizations in Japan is a direct result of Kathy Dennison's use of this process. When meeting Andy Bogen in Guam to pitch him on this business, Andy told us she tacitly refused for one hour to even discuss the opportunity. Finding her approach so refreshing and devoid of pressure, he then asked her to explain the business to him.

Secondly, experience has taught us that we really don't want people in power MLM who don't lose sleep over this opportunity. The people you want go home, lose sleep, and call you the next morning. Frequently, those who want to sign up at the first interview are people who will get "buyer's remorse," cool on the program, and drop out in a short time. We would rather have this happen before we've spent exhaustive time training them or signing them up and taking their money. The best time to lose people is *before* you sign them up and train them, not *after*.

This option isn't for everyone. But if you use forbidden fruit up front, you must also reinforce your firm stand at the close. Say something like, "*Look, after you lose sleep over this tonight, call me up tomorrow and I **will** sign you up.*"

□□□

All of these steps for the initial interview fit and work neatly together. Some of you will be tempted to read this chapter, pick and choose what you think works best and throw the rest out.

Let us just tell you this. In our experience, the primary difference between those who failed and those who succeeded was that those who failed spent a lot of time trying to reinvent the wheel. They thought just because they were successful in some other form of free enterprise, they knew more than anybody else. Before they knew it they were back on the old forty year plan, driving back and forth to work like some poor old silly, sick, caged lion.

Don't let that happen to you. When you've earned $20,000 a month or more, then you can experiment. Treat this like the big business it is and be professional. Work at it during professional hours so that you don't give the impression it is just a little side line activity. Don't do presentations in bars on cocktail napkins, don't rent motel rooms, and don't get an office.

Start off following this advice step-by-step and before you know it, you and your family will have all the financial rewards you deserve and the freedom to enjoy it.

Let's review:

- The best place to have the opening interview and presentation is in a personal setting such as your home. The interview should not last more than an hour.

- Step one is the introductory phase. Explain to prospects what attracted you to this industry. Describe your situation and financial struggles. Share the fears you experienced and give your personal philosophy.

- Step two establishes credibility. Use magazine and newspaper articles that describe your company and products.

- Step three shows how the trends pervading our society have much to do with the momentum being experienced in our industry: wanting off the forty year plan, desire for security, Baby Boomers as trend setters.

- Step four is the shock phase. Here you verbally represent the huge potential financial rewards of your business opportunity. Develop a strong but true contrasting story of those who have stayed with traditional business only to become destitute in the end. Explain the huge income of someone in your upline.

- Step five is the media phase in which you use a video or audio tape production to explain facts about the company and its products. Preferably use a video. If the company doesn't provide them (though most good ones do), get them from people in your upline. Distributor-created videos are better than corporate recruiting tapes.

- During step six, the board presentation, explain your company's compensation plan, how a person can reach the pinnacle of success and how exponential growth works to create that success.

- When explaining exponential growth, use good limiting factors to illustrate, under real conditions, how easy it is to earn big dollars. Be truthful about the effects of attrition and limited sales.

- You must use examples of big dollars to attract already successful people to power MLM. Use the 5x5 example or "the millionaires club" or both.

- Step seven is the question-and-answer period. Avoid negative questions that distract from the focus of the big money and free time. Stress the support and proven track record available in your organization.

- Step eight is the close: Joining your company provides one with the ability to (1) purchase superior products at cost; (2) enjoy all the tax benefits of owning your own business, including worldwide travel and inheritance; and (3) build your own business with unlimited potential and passive residual income. Invite them to training.

- The next 24 hours are critical to the recruit because of self-doubt and negativism from skeptics. Recruits need material to take home to deal with negativism.

- An optional addition to the steps is to take the pressure off by saying you refuse to sign up the recruits unless they lose sleep or are terribly excited about it.

- Don't try to reinvent the wheel. Network Marketing is unique, and it is big business. Follow these steps and don't try to pick and choose elements before you have reached a high level of success. The risks are too great.

Chapter 7

Sponsoring New Distributors

Sponsoring new Marketing Associates is the lifeline of our business. Until you attain your own personal goal, never stop sponsoring. Most failures in this business are due to Distributors moving out of the recruiting mode into a management mode once they have built an organization. Don't fall into the management trap. Devote the largest portion of your time to recruiting and sponsoring. Support your new Marketing Associates by helping them get started right. Support your older Associates by helping them close prospects as they request it. Devote almost no time to prodding people along. You can't drag anyone in this business across the finish line. The secret to this business is recruit, recruit, recruit, and instill that philosophy in your downline. Never let a day go by without prospecting several people. Prospecting *enough* people is the key to successful sponsoring.

Signing up a new Distributor is easiest if done in teamwork with your sponsor or upline executives. The strength of new

Marketers is exemplified by the quality and quantity of their contacts and the credibility carried with each of them. So it is their job to plant the seed with their sphere of influence. The strength of the upline leaders is their experience and longevity in the company. So it is the leaders' job to offer support by watering that seed with 3-way calls or directly closing prospects for the new Marketing Associate on the phone.

Support often comes by way of addressing people's fears. In Network Marketing, more than any other industry, you must immunize yourself against negativity. Human nature expects to find something wrong before it can accept something as right. You must protect yourself against the *dreamstealers* and naysayers.

"Every free-spirited being is opposed by a thousand people who have been appointed to guard the past." Having others question the integrity of your business ... whether they have thought it through ... whether it is right for them ... what others will think of them if they participate—all of this is an integral part of this business. Don't be surprised by it. Be prepared for the fact that quality people will do a significant amount of analysis.

Preparing for Objections

Objections are really a lack of information—just unanswered questions. Don't let this intimidate you. Everyone you meet will have questions and some objections that need to be overcome. Here are some things you can do to help:

1. **Hear them all the way out.** The most important thing you can do is listen. Don't interrupt in the middle of a question.

2. **Repeat it back to them.** After they have stated their question or objection, repeat it back to them so you

understand it and they are sure you know. If you don't know the answer, tell them so. The answer is as close as your telephone. Help them know that you had similar questions, and that you understand why they are curious.

3. **Question it.** As you go through the question, have them talk about it as much as possible to determine if it is a true question or if they are looking for a reason not to be interested. It is important to know if we need to pass on more information or if we need to find the real problem.

4. **Answer it.** Answer the question as completely as possible.

5. **Confirm it and get their agreement.** Once you feel you have answered their question or objection, confirm it with them and get their agreement that the question or objection has been resolved.

6. **Go to the commitment question.** When the objections have been cleared out of the way, get to the commitment questions or decision time. (Are they ready to be a Distributor, a retail customer or should we pass them by?) Remember that this is a new experience for them and that any question or objection they have is a concern that must be addressed before you can have 100% of their commitment.

Answering Objections

Here are a number of questions we often hear:

• *Isn't your company a pyramid?*
   Explain that your company sells real products to real people and pays a commission when product is ordered. A pyramid is a method of recruiting people where little

or no product is involved. People are paid for moving paper, not selling products. At your company, nobody makes money until product is ordered. You can make more or less money than the person who involved you in this business depending on how much product you sell and how much product your downline sells. All Fortune 500 companies are pyramids. In the IBM pyramid, for example, no one earns more than the top person there.

Legitimate Network Marketing companies are not pyramids! The real pyramid schemes are often found in corporations where there are thousands of workers and only one who can make it to the top of the pyramid. In such structures, those at the bottom are often laid off during tough times while the one at the top sees a bonus or salary raise. In Network Marketing, everyone has an equal opportunity to make it to the top and to have unlimited financial success.

Consider the following: *30 years ago many people believed that franchises were a scam, and the U.S. Congress came within 11 votes of banning franchising. Today one-third of our GNP comes from franchising. Where would America and the rest of the world be today without franchises?*

• *I'm just not the selling type.*
When you go to a good restaurant, what do you do? You tell your friends. The same is true of good products that you use. Your company pays people for telling others about great products, not selling them. This type of selling is the natural result of enthusiasm for a great product line. If you are selling products that you use, your own personal transformations will boost your sales as friends notice the change. For once, the old cliché is

true: The product sells itself because the main product is you—your own new look or behavior. People will look at you and say to themselves: I want that for myself. Particularly the people you've known for years will be lining up to ask you to share your secret. And when you share, you "sell." So "selling" isn't really *selling*. It's not that most people can't sell, it's that they are afraid of rejection. Help them understand that everyone won't be interested in your products—or anything else for that matter—but when you have the best products of their kind in the world, the products almost sell themselves. All you have to do is get people to try them. Your business is much less about *selling* and more about *sharing* a great product and opportunity with people you care about.

- ***I'm not the Network Marketing type.***
  Over the years Network Marketing has received a black eye because:

  A. Many MLM companies have gone out of business and left people hanging. Most Network Marketing companies don't make it beyond two years. Only one out of a thousand make it beyond five years. So explain that your company has been in business since _____ and is on target to become a _____ dollar company. Your company is here to stay and so is Network Marketing.

  B. Some companies are less than up-front when presenting the opportunity to others. Over the years some companies have promoted inviting people over to a home under whatever means were possible and then presenting them with the opportunity after the doors were locked. Network Marketing is coming of age. People-to-people selling is the most power-ful type of selling available today. Your company does not promote any presentation method that makes the prospect feel uncomfortable. You do promote professionalism, honesty and hard work.

- ***I just don't have the money.***
  The Harvard Business School has as its definition of an Entrepreneur: "The pursuit of opportunity without re-gard to the financing of that opportunity." That is, you can always get the money. Success is desire over ob-stacles. Generally, those who have this objection don't understand the impact of the opportunity you are offer-ing them. If the desire is great enough, finding the money is usually not the real problem. The whole point of my showing you the opportunity is making you the money that you don't have. If someone parked a new Lexus in front of your house, dangled the keys in front of you and said "For $200, it's yours," *could you find the money?* Great! Go *there* and get the money because the business opportunity being offered to you now is of far, far greater value than one Lexus.

- ***I don't have the time.***
  "I have to commit myself 100% and can't afford to divert my focus from the other things that I am doing." This is an important quality in a person. That commit-ment level is usually what makes the person successful. So explain the following: If you had time freedom, we wouldn't need to talk. Of course, you are too busy. That is what we are trying to help you change. This business isn't a sprint. It's a marathon. All we ask is for two hours a day of complete focus on this opportunity. The addi-tional commitment of time will follow the success. You

can't afford not to do this business. *Many people are so busy making a living they forget to make a life.* If you don't plan for the future, no one else will do it for you. The Baby Boomers cannot count on government subsidized retirement programs. While it was a small pittance of support for their parents' generation, it is not likely to be there for them at all. You had better find time to plan for your future.

- *I'm too old.*

  Maybe so—when's the funeral? Age simply doesn't matter in this business. Distributors range in age from their mid-teens to late eighties. If you are currently 90 years old or older, we have a special plan to bring you into this business. Age is a function of attitude—not of birthdays. You can fail or succeed at anything, at any age.

- *I don't know anybody.*

  Think again. Social psychologists tell us that by age 30 the average person knows over 2,000 people. And even if you just moved to a new community, simple and dynamic techniques exist to help you build your business. Your sponsor will show you how.

- *It's saturated.*

  Saturation is nothing more than an excuse because saturation is impossible with our product lines, especially if you are working with consumable products. Customers use up what they buy, and then they reorder. Saturation can't occur. Just look at the numbers. *If, for example, you represent personal care products, of the $68 billion U.S. market, point out what portion of that your company sold last year. It's minuscule!* Experts predict this market will more than triple by the end of the decade as

Baby Boomers become increasingly concerned about their health, well-being and personal appearance. Saturated? Most people haven't even heard the name of your company yet. And we're just talking about the United States, which accounts for just seven percent of the world's personal care market. Remember: *your company is going international, out to capture a share of that remaining 93% of the world market.*

- ***My spouse doesn't want me to do this.***
  Of course not—what did you expect? Your spouse hasn't seen what you've seen. Any spouse worth having wouldn't want you to waste your time on a worthless deal. But you've seen what you spouse hasn't seen. Far from being worthless, our business is an opportunity for wealth, and more important, for time freedom. Once your spouse understands what this is all about, you'll have an essential ally in building your business. Now don't make the mistake of believing it will be easy to show your spouse what you have already seen. Get the spouse on a 3-way call.

- ***I'm not interested.***
  I can understand. This business isn't for everyone. But just to clarify my understanding, which is it you're not interested in—the unlimited money opportunity or the free time? (Wait for their laughter or other response.) They may then give one of the above objections. *If you can't close them, try to make them a retail customer and ask for referrals.*

- ***I want to think it over.***
  I can appreciate that. You wouldn't want to take the time to think it over unless you were seriously interested

in this, would you? Just to clarify my thinking, what exactly do you want to think over? Is it the company, the sales compensation plan, the products?

For any objection presented to you, these points are helpful:

A. Identify the advantages your company has to offer, namely, ongoing income and time freedom.

B. Help your prospect talk about what advantages your business offers to them.

C. Relate your own experiences. Explain how you got involved and the financial rewards you or your upline are experiencing.

D. Always be enthusiastic.

E. Refer often to the success others are having with this opportunity.

F. Mention how much you have learned since you joined the company (this will put your prospect at ease) and how presenting the opportunity and the knowledge about the product comes with time and experience.

G. Above all, remember to always reiterate the big money and free time. No one objects to $50,000 a month.

Finally, it is important to remember that sometimes you will hear objections from your prospect that don't sound logical. You will also find times when a prospect keeps putting off a decision. Don't waste your time trying to talk someone into the opportunity. If you can tell that they are looking for an excuse not to be involved, simply move on to the next prospect. Everyone won't be interested. This opportunity isn't for everyone. There are enough people who are excited and waiting for an opportunity to be presented to them that you don't need to waste time on those who aren't interested. Put them on your six-month callback list. Some of them will come in then when they see that you are still involved, committed and making money.

Once you have overcome the objections, and the prospect is ready to become your Distributor in business, keep the sign-up procedure simple and duplicable. A check list of what to do is highly recommended. Our suggestion for such a list is found in the Training Format section of the next chapter—the very first step, *Establishing your Business.*

Teaching a simple, duplicable system

Remember that everything you do is likely to be copied by your new Associates. Teach them a system that you want to be duplicated from the very first contact with them, but especially when you begin the sign-up. Teach them simple steps to:

1. Complete the application form, including an automatic delivery form if such a system is available to you;

2. Set up a temporary account with your company enabling them to order product and sales materials immediately while waiting for the paperwork to catch up;

3. Get started with product—a reasonable amount that they can easily use or share with their family and new Distributors;

4. Order the needed sales materials—just what they need in keeping with their business plan and no more;

5. Have them become acquainted with their upline and how to access them;

6. Make sure they establish a record keeping system to track customers, prospects, frontline and key downline Distributors, and, of course, expenses since you are now in business for yourself.

The Sign-up process

The sign-up process is one of the most legally sensitive aspects of Multi-Level Marketing. If our industry is questioned or looked upon with skepticism by any government, it is frequently with regard to the sign-up phase. They are concerned with such things as the volume requirements of a Distributor in order to be paid commissions on the downline; excessive product sales to a brand new Associate, or what we call in the business "front-end loading;" some are even concerned that any sign-up fee is required at all.

While we feel confident that these matters will be cleared up, there are certain precautions that Network Marketers could take that would greatly enhance the image of our industry. By far the most important is to avoid like the plague anyone who encourages a new Distributor to buy thousands of dollars worth of product. This practice has caused much heartache to some individuals and is the single worst infraction which gives a black-eye to our industry. We consider it a breech of ethics on the same par with downline switching, that is, encouraging someone to leave one organization and join another within the same company and with no waiting time as is mandated by most reputable companies.

You don't want to be a party to "front-end loading," neither as the perpetrator nor the victim. Don't let anyone convince you that such a "buy-in" will get you to *big money fast.* It can only get you to *big trouble fast* unless your company has a solid, unconditional long-term return policy.

With such a refund policy in place, what is an acceptable practice for some Distributors who intend to move on a fast track in the business is to purchase enough product to get their front line Marketers started with promotional volume. That presumes a fair degree of certainty that the new Associate will have people to sponsor, and can afford the purchase. In our company, for example, five active frontline Distributors are required in order to submit a letter of intent to pursue executive status. Therefore, for such a person who plans to become an executive and is assured of having others join his organization, we permit them to order five kits to have on hand for their first five sign-ups, once we are absolutely convinced the person is a winner. Usually we do this shortly after signing up the new Distributor.

This promotional volume is often what escalates a new Distributor into qualification, but should be distinguished from real volume—product ordered and reordered month after month by satisfied customers and Distributors who use and love the product. It is *real* volume, not *promotional* volume, that ultimately creates passive residual income and is the essence of what makes Network Marketing a viable, ongoing business.

Some Power Marketers, in their eagerness to get off to a fast start, simply don't understand this philosophy and will make the mistake of skipping over the critical step of creating real volume in their organizations. It is vital that new Marketers begin with a solid commitment to use as much product as possible, share the product personally—just among close family and friends—and teach everyone in their organization to do the same. As simplistic as this seems, this must be done before beginning the more dramatic and gratifying process of creating large promotional volume through your power players and teaching them to duplicate the process. It is the balance of both types of volume, promotional—to propel you into success in the early days, and real—to stabilize your volume and provide ongoing, residual income that offers you long-term success. Promotional volume is extremely valuable, but your business can survive without it. However, failure to create real volume can lead to the ultimate collapse of your organization.

Let's review:

- Until you attain your own personal goals, never stop sponsoring. The secret to this business is recruit, recruit, recruit, and instill that philosophy in your downline.

- Signing up a new Distributor is easiest if done in teamwork. It is the job of the new Marketer to plant the seed with their contacts. It is the job of the upline to water that seed by helping close prospects.

- Objections are really a lack of information—just unanswered questions. Don't let this intimidate you.

- Here are some guidelines to follow:
  1. Hear them all the way out.
  2. Repeat it back to them.
  3. Question it.
  4. Answer it.
  5. Confirm it and get their agreement.
  6. Go to the commitment question.

- *Isn't your company a pyramid?* A pyramid is a method of recruiting people where little or no product is involved. At your company, nobody makes money until product is ordered.

- *I'm just not the selling type.* Your business is much less about *selling* and more about *sharing* a great product and opportunity with people you care about. It is the natural result of enthusiasm for products you love.

- *I'm not the Network Marketing type.* Network Marketing is coming of age. People-to-people selling is the most powerful type of selling available today. You do so through professionalism, honesty and hard work.

- *I just don't have the money*. If someone parked a new Lexus in front of your house, dangled the keys in front of you and said "For $200, it's yours," *could you find the money*? Great! Go *there* and get the money because the business opportunity being offered to you now is of far, far greater value than one Lexus.

- *I don't have the time.* If you had time freedom, we wouldn't need to talk. Of course, you are too busy. That is what we are trying to help you change.

- *I'm too old.* Maybe so—when's the funeral? Age simply doesn't matter in this business.

- *I don't know anybody.* Social psychologists tell us that by age 30 the average person knows over 2,000 people.

- *It's saturated.* Saturation is impossible if you are working with consumable products. Customers use up what they buy, and then they reorder.

- *My spouse doesn't want me to do this*. Of course not—what did you expect? Your spouse hasn't seen what you've seen. Any spouse worth having wouldn't want you to waste your time on a worthless deal. But you know that this is far from worthless.

- *I'm not interested.* I understand, but just to clarify my thinking, what is it you are not interested in—the big money or the free time? (Wait for a chuckle and then you will usually hear their real objection remaining.

- *I want to think it over*. Just to clarify my thinking, what exactly do you want to think oer: Is it the company, the sales compensation plan, the products?

- Don't waste your time trying to talk someone into the opportunity. If you can tell they are looking for an excuse, simply move on the next prospect.

- Keep the sign-up procedure simple and duplicable. A check list of what to do is highly recommended.

- The sign-up process is one of the most legally sensitive aspects of Multi-Level Marketing. The most significant precaution Network Marketers can take is to avoid encouraging a new Distributor to buy thousands of dollars worth of product. This is the single worst infraction which gives our industry a black eye.

- What is an acceptable practice for some Distributors who intend to move on a fast track is to purchase enough product to get their front line Marketers started with promotional volume.

- Promotional volume is larger quantities ordered to have on hand for your new Associates. It is often what escalates a new Distributor into qualification. Real volume, on the other hand, is product ordered and reordered month after month by satisfied customers and Distributors who use and love the product.

- Some Power Marketers, seeing it as too simplistic, make the mistake of skipping over the critical step of creating real volume in their organizations. They rush into the more dramatic and gratifying process of building and duplicating promotional volume. Promotional volume is extremely valuable, but without real volume, can lead to the ultimate collapse of your organization.

Chapter 8

Training and Support

There is really no magic in training and supporting your downline. The fact is, Multi-Level Marketing is easy as far as the technical ins and outs of the business are concerned.

However, the difficulties in MLM are things you can't teach—such as self-starting, following a winning pattern, keeping motivated, and coping with rejection. Of course, you will offer hints, but you might as well accept the fact that you cannot lead these people by the hand through every step to success. If you try, you will be lost because you will have to ignore your own business to do it. What's more, you will not be doing the recruits any favors by spending too much time on training or holding their hands as a means of support.

As any good psychologist will tell you, if you let people rely on you too heavily in seeing through a project or any other endeavor, you create a cripple who is constantly in need of support rather than being able to rely on his or her own devices. Do not make cripples out of your Associates. Remember—you cannot drag anyone across the finish line.

Finally, do not use training and extensive formal support procedures as an excuse for not doing your real work. We've seen a number of people fail at Network Marketing because they became enamored with the easier and more secure training and support aspects of the business and stopped recruiting. They built up grandiose and lofty ideas about their training and support efforts only to find themselves in the position of having no one to train and support. There is an axiom used in almost all successful sales organizations: "The day you stop cold calling is the day you start to fail." A similar axiom for MLM is this: "The day you stop *recruiting* is the day you start to fail," at least during the first three years or until you have achieved your goals.

That said, you still must provide some training and some amount of support to your downline. If you don't, you'll reduce the chances of those below raising themselves to your level of success. You want them to be as successful, or more so.

Two underlying goals must direct your efforts in training and support:

First is balance. We should strive for balance in every part of our lives. We all need the right amount of work, play, and rest. We need companionship, love, and solitude. Things seem to go awry in our lives when any part becomes out of balance with the others. The same is true in your work in MLM. But keep in mind that balance does not necessarily mean keeping each part in equal amounts. It only means keeping the parts in workable proportions. In this case you need to keep in proportion your purpose of building a large downline, with making sure individuals in the downline have what they need to succeed. Do not waste your time giving them things they do not need or spending an inordinate amount of time with those who are not going to succeed no matter what you do. You could better spend your time recruiting someone who will succeed and letting the sure failure—that guy who won't listen or try—fail.

The second underlying goal is to provide people with the facts they need to succeed, and arm them with the rules and procedures you know, to help them become successful power Marketers.

This second goal is extremely important because the quickest and surest way to power MLM success is for recruits to duplicate the methods of successful power Marketers. They cannot do this if you don't tell them how to duplicate you. Correspondingly, you must stress, over and over again, that recruits must duplicate your efforts and not deviate until they too have become successful. We have said this many times throughout the book, and you must do the same in your first training session.

The Training Session

To maintain balance between recruiting and training, recruit Monday through Friday, then hold a training session on Saturday. Of course, you won't do this fifty-two weeks a year. You will take some time off. Hold a training session for a new recruit within two to four days of the time he first signs up or shows an interest in signing up. You cannot allow too long a cooling-off period, and besides, you don't want recruits to forget everything they learned in the first interview.

Most of the training can be performed in a couple of hours. The first thing you should do as the training session begins is hand out a prepared outline or guide of what you are going to cover during the session.

If some people are late for the session, don't go back and repeat for them. Though that sounds a little traditional business oriented, keep in mind that though people are in MLM to avoid the problems of traditional business, we must still approach MLM in a professional manner. If people are chronically late, they make for an inefficient organization and take away from everyone else's efforts, if for no other reason than that you have to constantly repeat yourself. You simply do not have time to waste.

After you have handed out the outline, but before you go over it, give a talk on the importance of duplication, of avoiding maverick approaches, of how to follow your lead on the path to success. Explain strongly the fact that traditional business procedures, except in selected circumstances, have little to do with MLM success. Then go over the outline.

□□□

Training Format

The following outline is a summary of information needed to show new Distributors how to do this business. Until they have a successful track record of their own, teach them to closely follow this format, and not attempt to reinvent the Network Marketing wheel.

I. Establishing your Business

A. *Complete the Application form.*

This places you on the computer with your company and assigns you an identification number permitting you to sponsor other Distributors. If automatic delivery is offered in your company, encourage new Associates to complete this form and encourage others to do the same.

B. Set up a temporary account.

Since it takes several days for the application to reach the home office and be entered on the computer, setting up a temporary account or otherwise arranging for new Associates to be able to get product allows them to purchase product at wholesale cost immediately and is generally good for 30 days. In the case of long-distance sponsoring, reverse steps A and B. Close your prospect by calling into the company and setting up their temporary account. Then follow with the application and paper work.

C. Order product.

With your sponsor's help, place your first order for the Starter Kit and Product Package as recommended from your company. Although a product order is generally optional and a Starter Kit is the only requirement for becoming a Distributor, it is virtually impossible to begin your business without using and loving the product line. Depending upon the goals of the new Associate, you may offer both a *basic track* for those intending to become wholesale buyers or retailing Distributors and an *executive track* for those intending to build an organization in the company. Basic track should meet volume requirements for being an active Distributor. Executive track meets volume requirements for pursuing a leadership breakaway position in the company.

D. Order the tools of the business.

Purchase the necessary items including application/agreement forms, product order forms, corporate and product brochures, etc. Upon the advice of your sponsor, select training materials, available through your company or upline, that will teach you proven methods of retailing product and enrolling new Network Marketers into your business. If none are provided through your company or organization, see the last page of this book for generic materials available to you through us.

E. *Know your Upline*

Get the names and phone numbers of those people upline from you who have a vested interest in your success. As you come to know their various backgrounds and personal strengths, work with those who are most able to give you the support you need. You will create a bond with certain ones. This is a vital step in this business, as you will quickly come to learn. You cannot succeed in this type of business alone. It is an expected and intrinsic part of the system to lean on upline for support in closing your star prospects. MLM is a business of team effort.

F. *Order Voice Mail*

Voice mail is the heartbeat of Network Marketing. If you are in the business for the purpose of building a downline (as opposed to merely using or retailing the product), then you will want to order the voice mail program available through your company. This is a unique and interesting innovation that allows us to communicate with each other. It allows you to be on a voice network hearing from company representatives, your sponsor and upline executives. Messages can be passed conveniently and easily about such things as where opportunity and training meetings are being held, new updated information tips for effectively working your business, and other information that needs to be passed quickly among your group.

G. *Set up your phone system*

Set up your answering machine or local voice mail system with a businesslike message. Order three-way conference calling. This and a voice messaging system should be available through your local phone company.

H. *Set up a record keeping system.*

Set up a system for tracking your customers and another for tracking your prospects and new Associates. This can be done on index cards or a computer. Finally keep a daily journal of your business expenses. Now that you are self-employed, you will have many tax advantages not previously available to you if you were exclusively employed by a company. In most instances, these are the only records you will need to keep. All other paperwork is done by the company, leaving you free to do the people work.

II. Product Usage

All successful Network Marketers are "products of the product." It is essential that new Distributors be taught to commit to use and introduce everyone in their families to your entire product line. Also, by placing your products strategically throughout your home, guests will naturally be encouraged to try them and some will become customers. Remember, everyone who wishes to succeed in this business must begin by understanding the products you sell. That understanding comes from usage. Seriously question the commitment of anyone who is unwilling to change his family over to the products used by your company. And above all else remember this—even if Distributors quit recruiting and selling your products, you want to keep them on line as active customers.

III. Retail Sales

A legitimate Network Marketing company is concerned primarily with moving products from the producer to the consumer. All leaders should begin by selling some products, thereby demonstrating leadership by example. Most leaders will focus on showing the business plan to prospects, and build a retail base from those who reject the business opportunity but show interest in the product. The following are some suggestions for effective retailing.

1. Begin by exposing all of your relatives to your products. For example, Mark sent products to his relatives with an invoice and a note explaining his new business. Then he preceded the mailing by telephoning them and requesting that they use the products for a week after which they could either send him a check or return the products. Thirteen became regular retail customers.

2. As a Distributor, carry samples of your products with you wherever you go. Hand them out to everyone who appears interested. Explain that you have found them to be the best products in the world and you would like to become their personal representative. Get their business card or home number and call them back for an order within four days.

3. Always send prospective Distributors home from your recruiting interviews with product samples. Every person who sees this opportunity should, at the very least, be given the opportunity to become a customer.

IV. Goal Setting

Success is having worthwhile goals and taking the necessary steps to achieve them. As long as you are taking steps, you are successful. Network Marketing is merely a vehicle. People who have purpose driven business plans, who truly understand why they are in this business and where they want it to take them, are far more effective in business than those who do not. Obviously, the more committed and dedicated you are to your purpose, the more on track you will stay with this business. Therefore, we strongly suggest that every goal you set must be achievable, measurable, specific and written down. It must be achievable so you know it's worth the effort to get started. It must be measurable so you will know when you are succeeding and when you need to put in more effort. It must be specific so you know whether you are hitting your target. Finally, it must be written so you will be less likely to change your mind while on the path. The entire chapter three is dedicated to helping you accomplish this.

V. Prospecting and Recruiting

Prospecting is the very foundation of Network Marketing. Once you have set written goals, and created an action plan based on specific numbers of people you will approach and specific methods for prospecting and recruiting in both your warm and cold markets, you are ready to take the next step.

A. Begin immediately compiling a list of 2,000 names of friends, relatives, acquaintances and associates. Use a telephone directory and book of vocations to help you recall them. It seems like a tall order but social psychologists have proven repeatedly that, by the age of thirty, the average person knows 2,000 people on a first name basis. We resisted this at first but were able to come up with 1,700 names when we used these memory-triggering tools.

B. Next, call those people on your warm list and invite them in groups of eight or ten to your home for a presentation. When calling to invite them, mention only big money and free time. You *must* avoid the temptation to discuss your company until they arrive at your home. At that time, you will tell them all about your product and opportunity. Although the average top leaders earn much more than this, be flexible in using income figures that are believable but beyond their current income. Here is an example of what you might say :

"Jim, you're not going to believe what my wife and I have taken on. We are more excited about this than anything we have seen in our entire adult lives and with the caliber of people involved in this, we thought of you right away. We are talking about thirty to fifty thousand a month and all the free time you've ever wanted!"

Remember, half will not show up unless you are very firm in getting them to commit to the meeting. None will show up if you insist on telling them about the product or opportunity over the telephone. This warm market prospecting could take from two to four months.

C. When you have exhausted your warm market, set a goal to begin working in your cold market talking to twenty or thirty prospects each day. The best approach, after breaking the ice with small talk, is this:

"I've got to ask you a wild question but I'd like a serious answer. If you knew for sure that you could earn twenty to thirty thousand dollars a month and retire in three years at that income level, would that excite you?"

Those who answer "yes" are prospects. Simply request their card and tell them you will be calling to set up an interview. No matter how persistent they may be in requesting additional information, don't give it. Just get their card and tell them you are on your way to another meeting.

D. Once you're ready, your sponsor will assist you in telephoning a few people in your warm market as well as preparing you for cold calling.

VI. The Presentation

Each business opportunity presentation should be highly duplicable. Your sponsor will teach you the board illustrations and you will become familiar with them very quickly. Even those who are very intimidated by public speaking will find this presentation comfortable and nonthreatening. Chapter five describes this step in full, but here is an outline of the steps to follow:

A. Hand out one or two pieces of literature as people arrive—perhaps a company brochure or some magazine article reprint about Network Marketing.

B. Briefly tell your story, why you are involved. Describe your life in terms of stress, traffic, making someone else wealthy, building no future security, etc. At some point be sure and mention that you were impressed by the upside potential of the earnings of people already succeeding in your company. Also mention the fact that you were impressed with the opportunity for time freedom.

C. Stress the credibility of our industry, your company, your particular organization and your products by referring to the handouts you gave them when they came in.

D. Talk about the huge potential rewards strongly and accurately. Site specific figures of average earnings or tell a story about one of your mentors in your company.

E. Show a company video of your choice—preferably the

one you saw at your first presentation, which tells them about the company and the product. Be sure to explain how social trends are supporting the need for our industry, if your video does not do this.

F. Present the board illustrations. Your sponsor will demonstrate them for you.
   • the compensation plan
   • 5 x 5 x 5 scenario
   • the millionaires club

G. Field all their questions.

H. Give them samples, an audio tape, and invite them to the next Saturday training.

I. Be certain that as they prepare to leave, you give the three compelling reasons to become a Distributor with your company:
   a. Wealth and time freedom
   b. Tax advantages
   c. Wholesale purchase of superior products

VII. The Sign Up

We always sign people up for the basic start-up cost. Then we recommend a product starter package which provides the most frequently used products. We recommend that the total start up costs stay very reasonable—no more than three or four hundred dollars. You might encourage Distributors on the basic track to begin with $100 of redirected spending and complete the automatic delivery form if available to you. Some people who sincerely prove to us that they can do this business and are on the executive track are permitted to purchase several starter packages. But they have to be able to demonstrate exceptional leadership skills because we refuse to front-end-load new Distributors.

VIII. Training

Use this format and cover the ten points you are being taught right now. This represents a summary training of the most important elements for doing this business, and can be taught in one hour. Those who choose to do more than one training session should use the "First Step Training" followed by a one-on-one "Personal Training" once the first steps have been completed. Both can be found in our *Encyclopedia of Network Marketing* and are more detailed in explaining key concepts. Either approach means that these ten points are clearly covered before your new Associate begins working the business. This book with our tape series provides basic training.

IX. Support

While it's important to always recognize that leaders cannot be created, nor can anyone be "dragged across the finish line," you must be prepared to support those who seek your guidance, irrespective of which level in your group they occupy. Support your enthusiastic leaders, by telephone primarily, and always be ready to assist them when they request it. Follow this simple rule of thumb: if they contact you and sincerely request your assistance, always stand ready to help them. What you should not do is call and pester them or prod them to place orders. Don't attempt to magically convert them into leaders. Real leaders will seek you out. Our experience is that you create dependency and weakness when you attempt to do this business *for y*our people. Strong support means being there at all times for your key people and always assisting them in developing self-sufficient leadership skills.

Above all else, don't fall victim to the management trap. You aren't a manager. You are a recruiter and trainer who is looking for leaders who can manage themselves. Give them the tools to succeed; then get out of their way and drop the ego need to take credit for their success. Remember, success has a hundred fathers and failure is an orphan.

X. Commitment

Commit to do this business for two to three years and never allow yourself to get sidetracked by dream stealers or negative people. Remember every great Network Marketer was a lousy Network Marketer at first. Success in Network Marketing results more often from attitude than ability, and commitment is one of the most important attitudes. *If your goal is to become a leader, you will want to notify your company as quickly as possible—preferably in your first month—that you are on track to become an Executive. This is often done in the form of a Letter of Intent (LOI).* Remember, the first few months you'll likely be the most underpaid professional in the world. But if you persevere and put forth the effort, following these steps, you will eventually feel like the most overpaid professional in the world.

□□□

In the outline, place heavy emphasis on the lists of steps taken from this book, focusing on how these steps are all directed to only one thing: building the large, solid downline necessary to power MLM success. You may want to use this book in your training, or order our training manual, *The Encyclopedia of Network Marketing.* It contains a complete training manual and audio cassette series on how to do this business.

The first stage of training is perhaps the most mundane but is extremely important for the duplication process. Explain the little details of the company such as how to get training materials and other resources; what programs are available through your company, such as voice mail, retailing programs, satellite access; whom to contact on payment problems; and any specific details of doing business, such as applications or automatic withdrawal forms. These facts are important. The best way to do this is to prepare a handy check list for recruits as suggested in the outline. You will still have to go over it during the training session, but you will save a lot of time by having it on paper.

Take time to thoroughly go over your company's compensation plan. Though you have gone over this before in the interview and presentation, go over it again, this time in more detail. This is the most important part of MLM for the new Distributors. One of the things you will want to explain in more depth on your board presentation, is your company's "roll-up" system, if such a system exists in your company. Roll-ups take people off the roster of Distributors and subsequently out of the reward systems once they have actually stopped working, thus allowing others who are successful below them to roll-up to you.

The roll-ups are important to new recruits as both a carrot and a stick. There was a time in Network Marketing when all a person had to do was sign up, sit back, and draw money off of other people's efforts. That, of course, diluted the available money to those who were actually producing. Nowadays, most good companies take non-producers (or buyers) out of the system, so that those who do produce get the rewards. For new recruits this means they will get their fair share of the pot if they work, but they won't if they don't.

Finally, let us share this caution about one of the most infuriating aspects of training. Invariably one, if not several new Distributors at the session, feel compelled to share their personal business histories with everyone else. They want to talk war stories, past problems, or about their deep and abiding insights into successes and failures. No matter what you say they will try to twist it to some specific story of their own.

Of course, we can all learn from each other, but usually these people and their stories waste a lot of time. Often they have such a high opinion of how much they know about everything, that you find your training session stalled and disrupted. People like this rarely change. Here is a suggestion for handling this situation.

Before people start talking to a disruptive degree, with the understanding that there will always be a little, tell them up front that history is irrelevant, that we all are embarking on new lives. When a session begins to deteriorate due to this problem, remark, "how interesting," then restate the importance of moving ahead in the session and your lives. After the training session, when everyone goes out to conquer the world, try to avoid those people because if you don't, and if they haven't stopped it, you will risk their monopolizing your time. Big talkers are seldom big doers.

Support

The keys to effectively supporting your downline in power Multi-Level Marketing revolve as much around what not to do as what to do.

This is because in a good portion of the MLM industry, a misleading notion has evolved that suggests that individual Distributors need constant attention, hand-holding, and ego boosting. This may be true with organizations that rely heavily on part-timers (which we'll cover) but it is an opposite approach to what we've found successful. You want to teach them a duplicable system and let them go. Teach downline to call upline when they need your support. And then be there for them when they call.

The fact is, the type of people you are recruiting for power MLM would be offended by the innumerable and insufferable rah-rah meetings you hear and read about so often. $15,000,

$25,000, $50,000 a month is its own good reward, for most serious Marketers.

Distributors dedicated primarily to retailing will often respond to acknowledgments even more than those who are building an organization. Although, from time to time, recognition is appreciated by everyone. "Babies cry for it and grown men die for it."

On the issue of meetings, most sponsors try to hold too many. Many people in MLM suggest that you hold regular meetings on a weekly or bi-weekly basis. What for?

Again, is it to keep people pumped? Is it to provide some sort of support group? Beyond once a month or so, we find meetings to be a distraction from doing the business, and so will your recruits who truly get the point of power MLM. You'll find that the good recruits simply will not need you much after a few weeks because they are spending their time doing the same thing you are—recruiting.

With the periodic meetings you do choose to hold, make sure your purpose is to be supportive to your organization. Some leaders hold weekly hotel meetings in order to sift through the friends of their new recruits. Then when they and the others fail, those leaders get all the roll-ups. This self-serving approach to MLM is one that good leaders don't encourage.

We've found that the best way to support your downline, besides leading by example, is to use the telephone for troubleshooting, and helping to close their prospects. We believe that *closing is the single most important thing a sponsor and/or an upline can do to support their people*. Until the new Associate has achieved a good income level, upline should assist in closing power prospects.

There are essentially three ways a sponsor or upline executive/direct can be supportive to their organization:

   1. Through voice messaging

2. By taking personal calls
3. By doing meetings

Voice Messaging is an easy and convenient way for a leader to talk to the entire downline organization or specific groups within it with one phone call. It generally saves time and money and avoids the endless game of telephone tag. Among other things it serves:

1. To let the downline know about the new training and recruiting materials such as video and audio tapes, magazine articles, and testimonials;
2. To disclose any changes in company personnel or policies;
3. To discuss any problems in payments or deliveries;
4. To exchange new ideas on expansion in product sales and recruiting areas;
5. To introduce any new products;
6. To send uplifting messages intended to motivate and encourage members of the organization.

Personal Calls are a major part of support. Associates are encouraged to call as often as they need help. But *they* must call. That's how you know that they are serious about the business. Your group will eventually grow to the point that you cannot initiate calls to everyone in your organization. Teach your Distributors to call *up* when they are *down* and to call *down* only when they are *up*. An Associate should expect support, and not be intimidated to call upline, for two prime reasons:

1. To discuss specific problems and necessary changes in their approach—if they are really working;
2. To help close a prospect through a direct or three-way call.

You can do ninety percent of your troubleshooting over the phone, save time wasted on meetings, and go about the business of your recruiting or, better yet, spend more time playing.

Meetings are not needed often, but they do serve a purpose:

1. To periodically present the business opportunity to your downline and downlines' prospects;
2. To offer training, updating the organization on new information or getting them back on track on old systems;
3. To support your group by your presence, especially if you don't live in the same town;
4. To bond your organization to each other and to you;
5. To acknowledge Associates in your organization for special achievements.

Recognition is an extremely important facet of this business. Beyond the money and lifestyle, many people are in Network Marketing because it gives them a sense of belonging. This becomes a substitute or second family. Acknowledging people for their accomplishments and successes, no matter how small, is a constructive part of upline support.

Then too, you are going to find that you make new friends of some of your frontline and even some of the downline as you meet them. You will naturally spend time with them.

The key to all the support is this: Accept the fact that some of your front and downlines will fail, if that's their choice. As much as you would like to, you can't drag them across the finish line. Often it will save you more time and money to let someone fail and recruit another who will succeed. Even if the failing person is your friend, he or she will understand if that person is truly your friend. Leaders have to be found: they can't be created. Whatever you do, always remember that the only way for you to succeed is to make sure you have that large organization to support and train. You won't have anyone to support if you don't have the downline.

Let's review:

- You must know what you can and cannot do for recruits. You cannot teach self-starting, motivation, and how to cope with rejection. You can only hint.

- If you try too hard to lead recruits through every step and every problem, you risk creating cripples and you ignore your own business.

- Two goals should direct all your efforts in training and support. The first is for you, the second for recruits:
  1. Try to attain balance between your own recruiting and supporting your downline.
  2. Provide facts and tools so your downline can succeed.

- Most training can be accomplished in one 2-hour session.

- You must hold a training session for new recruits within two to four days of when they first sign up.

- First step in the training session is to hand out an outline of what you will cover.

- Do not let people in the session get out of hand. If they are late, tell them not to be. Keep them from telling their own personal stories. Explain that all that is past is history and then get on with it.

- In the outline place emphasis on building a huge downline.

- The outline should cover:
  1. Establishing your business: getting set up.
  2. Product usage: be a product of the product.
  3. Retailing product: share the products with everyone you know.

4. Setting Goals: have a purpose driven business plan.
5. Prospecting and recruiting: invite everyone to look at the opportunity.
6. The presentation: tell your story and show them how the plan works.
7. The sign up: sponsor new Associates at reasonable start-up costs.
8. Training: teach them the information following this outline.
9. Support: encourage Distributors to become leaders, while giving support to those who ask.
10. Commitment: notify the company of your intent to become a breakaway executive/direct, and stay with it for 2 to 3 years.

• Take extra time to explain the company's compensation plan and system of "roll-ups."

• Make a list of the company's procedures for getting started and hand it out. The list should include who to contact on payment problems, necessary forms, etc.

• The key to support is knowing what not to do as much as knowing what to do. Teach a duplicable system and let them go. Have downline call upline, but don't pester your Distributors.

• Most power Marketers do not need constant support, rah-rah meetings, and other ego boosters. Big bucks are their best reward. Retailing Distributors most appreciate recognition and from time to time, everyone likes to be acknowledged for special achievement.

• Hold meetings to a minimum: no more than once a month or so.

- There are three ways an upline can be supportive:
  1. Through voice messaging
  2. By taking personal calls
  3. By doing meetings

- Voice Messaging is a convenient way for an upline to support his or her entire organization.

- Personal calls are best used for troubleshooting and helping to close prospects for your Distributors.

- Meetings held periodically give leaders the chance to support their organization, bonding the members together as a group and offering recognition to those who have achieved special accomplishments.

- Support is not unconditional. Accept the fact that people will fail if that is their choice. Don't spend too much time on someone who is bound to fail. You must keep building your organization. It is better to let go of failures and recruit people who will succeed. Leaders have to be found; they can't be created.

Part III

Part-Time
Multi-Level Marketing

Chapter 9

The Part-Time
Multi-Level Marketer

Perhaps it is a misnomer of sorts to have this book titled *Power Multi-Level Marketing* and still include this section on part-time, more product-focused, MLM. Here's why we decided to do it. In conversations with heavy hitters—people like Richard Kall and others, one of the things we discuss is the manner in which many are recruited into Network Marketing. We never felt compelled to hoodwink people into this business. In fact, one of the things that concerned all of us, the single thing that had given MLM a bad name and dispirited new recruits, was the practice of using power Marketers' checks to recruit people whose only intention was to work part time at their business.

The fact is you cannot make the big bucks that heavy hitters make by working at it with part-time retailing methods. However, we place no value judgment on the distinction between power and part-time methods. In our downline of fifty thousand plus, many are part-timers and are successful as well. The point is, their success is defined differently, and the path to success must be approached differently. Drawing distinctions is extremely important so that all involved in MLM can reap tremendous rewards reasonably, intelligently, and honestly. Unfortunately, other publications and many recruiters never draw distinctions, yet they are so very necessary.

What to Expect Out of Part-Time MLM

The financial rewards on any level of MLM can be astounding, and for the part-timer this can be particularly true. However, don't expect to make the $25,000 to $100,000 a month that power Marketers make. It just won't and can't happen. Sure, there have been a few lucky cases, and after a few years, a power Marketer will usually cut back his hours and work part time. But for 99.9 percent of the people who start out using the part-time approach, those huge numbers won't happen.

However, a part-timer *can* reasonably expect to earn $500 to $5000 a month, often working as little as three hours a week. A minister friend in Michigan who is in our downline has been earning over $700 a month since his third month for the past year and a half. Yet he has never worked more than three hours a week and hasn't signed up anyone for the past six months.

In addition to his full-time salary, that's not bad. That is two extra car payments every month. Or it is the grocery and utility money. For many people, such outside income can be used for investment money, for retirement, or for "toys" such as a boat or a summer house. It can be used for a child's college education or personal fulfillment for a spouse who has never before worked outside the home but now feels a need to contribute income to the family.

Acquiring or accomplishing any of these goals can provide benefits to any person or family. Once accomplished, it can be viewed as success. The distinction, however, is that they are limited accomplishments, or they are specific accomplishments gained in pursuit of limited goals. That is the major overriding distinction between power and part-time MLM. The power Marketer has unlimited goals. The part-timer has limited goals. Yet, as those goals are identified and met, the part-timer's goals may reasonably change and even expand.

We have even seen some part-timers' incomes reach the $3,000 to $5,000 a month range and more. Before we married and as a single parent, working about 25 hours a week, Rene worked her way up to $100,000 a year part time while serving in an elected office as County Commissioner. Many people can live on this kind of income, and sometimes part-timers will quit their jobs to live an easier life, just working a few hours a week. The headaches are few and there is plenty of time for relaxation. A few part-timers will switch and become power Marketers because they catch a vision of what they can accomplish through MLM, and their limited expectations change to a vision of unlimited potential.

No matter where the part-time approach takes a part-timer, as long as he has a clear understanding of what part-time MLM can do, and what his own expectations are, he can be very successful.

A Part-Timer's Profile

In our experience, there are three types of people who start their trek in MLM on a part-time basis. They are:

- People who continue their current work status, but who either want extra income or replacement income so they can leave their job and eventually come full-time into this business.
- People who prefer and are more comfortable with focusing their energy on product sales and building a cutomer base.

- People who can see the full potential of MLM but because of security fears or lack of confidence cannot or do not want to plunge into MLM with both feet by becoming a Power Marketer.

The first group, those who choose to continue their current work status, make up a significant part of our organization. Some of them plan to continue their work and are only interested in making some extra money. Though they will show significant growth for a time, it usually levels off suddenly as soon as they reach their goals. But their incomes are steady, and they can be counted on for a regular amount of production every month.

The people from this group can come from any walk of life. They are often homemakers who have not been seduced into the frantic pace of the business world, who thoroughly enjoy their role and position of making their home run smoothly. But they decide they need a little more money for their children's education, or for vacations, or to put away for retirement. Some merely use it, after their kids have left home or are older and involved in outside activities, as a way to fill spare time and meet new people.

Others who fit into this category are those who love their work and wouldn't give it up for the world. Almost everyone can use extra cash, and MLM on a part-time basis is a good way to get it.

Still others see the big picture, cannot afford to give up the cash flow of their current profession because of family responsibilities, but work the business with the same zeal as a Power Marketer. This group should follow the guidelines for a Power Marketer but with longer-term goals and realistic restrictions placed on their time. In their case, they would not follow the more product oriented part-time program. They ultimately plan to transfer over to being a Power Marketer as soon as they are able to replace their income. We recommend that this be sustained for at least a couple of months and that your growth outweighs your attrition.

The second group are people who are already using and always intend to use the company's products. They believe in them so much that they want their friends to use them. So why not make a little money on the side by selling them to friends or recruiting other friends to sell them?

The third group—those who see the bigger potential of MLM but for one reason or another cannot bring themselves to plunge into power MLM full time—pose problems for recruiters and themselves.

While we have castigated much of the industry for luring people in on a part-time basis with the power Marketers' checks, we also need to point out that this is not always the result of some sinister design on the recruiter's part. It's just that it's difficult to refrain from telling people what they want to hear or keep them from hearing only those things they want to hear.

We cannot tell you how many times we have interviewed a new recruit who can only see big dollar signs and still visualizes the megabucks coming to him while working only a couple of hours a week and still holding down a sixty-hour a week job.

Often, what these people hear us say is the vast amounts of money a person can make. They hear us describe the methods as simple and easy, really quite uncomplicated. What they do not hear us say is this: *Success in Multi-Level Marketing, whether part-time or full-time, depends on duplicating the efforts of those who have gone before you!*

It is extremely important to say this again especially to people who find themselves in this category. We are afraid of seeing people sign up expecting the money of a power Marketer while thinking they only have to put out part-time effort. They finally become disheartened or disenchanted and quit. They are a waste of any recruiter's time, they hurt the industry because they are often chronic complainers. But most important, they do a grave injustice to themselves. They place themselves in an impossible situation and give themselves, their families, and more likely, their colleagues a lot of grief when it isn't necessary.

With all that said, if you find yourself in this third category, be assured that you can be quite successful in part-time MLM and can still eventually reach your megabuck dreams if you keep these things in mind.

1. Part-time MLM is a good way to learn the business. While you will not achieve the power experience using part-time methods, there are enough similarities for you to gain much-needed experience. Though recruiting is not as intense, you still will learn recruiting techniques going part time. You will learn the inside and out of your product line. And you will have a list in place to begin should you ever decide to go the power route. You will have the advantage of having, though small, an organization already in place.

2. You will find it easier to deal with the real world of part-time MLM if you develop some smaller goals which will ultimately lead to the bigger goal of going full time. That is, set your sight buying new cars, or making house payments, or a vacation home, or a certain level of income until you are ready to make your break. As you meet one goal, establish new ones. And always evaluate and count your personal assets and achievements as you accomplish your goals.

3. Be willing to re-evaluate and adjust your thinking about Network Marketing as you work at it. You may find that you are actually quite satisfied with the rewards in comparison to your effort with your part-time work. However, if you do not adjust your longer range view or desires to come into line with the amount of effort you wish to expend, then you will be continually dissatisfied. We find that many people never make this adjustment, and it is at this point that they are tempted to quit. It just doesn't make sense.

If you keep and incorporate all these things into your mind set about Network Marketing, you will be in control of your own destiny by having a realistic understanding of what you can achieve. This kind of control over your own destiny will always make you successful no matter what level of Multi-Level Marketing you are in at a particular time.

One final note: With the exception of the part-timer striving to become a full-timer, there is a particular feature unique to part-time MLM that we find very appealing. It is this: people can, for all practical purposes, quit working at their business when they have reached an income level with which they are satisfied. But unlike a power Marketer whose life consists of continuous recruiting, a part-timer's focus on retail sales is usually stronger. Once a part-timer develops a solid customer base, the work can stop, except for attrition, because his income level is where he wants it. What a nice position to be in. You establish what you need and want, work to get there, and you stop (except for replacing the occasional customer who stops buying), leaving you more time to enjoy the extra income.

Let's review:

- Never use the checks of power Marketers to recruit people who only want to work part time.

- The goals of a part-timer are different, more limited, than those of a full-time Network Marketer. Thus, a part-timer's success must be defined differently. As long as a part-timer has a clear understanding of what he can accomplish with part-time MLM, and what his own expectations are, he can be very successful.

- A part-timer can reasonably expect to earn between $500 to $5000 per month and sometimes more.

- Three types of people enter MLM on a part-time basis:

  1. People who continue with their present occupations, but who need extra income or are working toward income replacement.
  2. People who prefer to focus on retail sales.
  3. People who see the full-time potential of MLM but, for security's sake, cannot bring themselves to plunge head first into MLM.

- Those who choose to continue with or are committed to their present occupations, often make the best part-timers because they more easily come to grips with their limited goals.

- Those who keep their profession but are striving for income replacement work the business like a Power Marketer but put in significantly less time—hoping eventually to become a Power Marketer.

- Those who focus on retail sales are usually in a program because they like and use the products.

- Those part-timers in the third group, who see the bigger picture of MLM but won't go into it full-time for security reasons, pose problems to themselves and upline.

- These people often are unhappy in their occupations and with part-time MLM. They often only hear what they want to hear; they see only the big dollar signs but refuse to believe that they cannot make them on a part-time basis. They often fail to come to grips with the fact that a person can only become successful with limited goals on a part-time basis.

- These security minded people must remember that success in MLM, whether part time or full time, depends on duplicating the efforts of those who have gone before.

- Here are three suggestions to help those in the second group understand that the high dollar rewards are still possible sometime later:

    1. Part-time MLM is a good way to learn the business.
    2. While pursuing part-time MLM, develop smaller goals with the ultimate intention of going full time as you see your success build. Set your sights on buying a new car, or making house payments. As you meet one goal, set new ones.
    3. Be willing to re-evaluate your ideas about MLM as you work with it. You might find that you are satisfied with the rewards you get while working a limited amount of time. If so, don't be afraid to give up the high-dollar long-term goal.

- With the exception of the part-timer striving to become a full-timer, an appealing feature of part-time MLM is that once a person reaches a satisfying income level, he can consider quitting, except for attrition.

Chapter 10

Basic Steps to
Part-Time MLM Success

Let's assume that you have come to grips with whatever goals you want to achieve in your Network Distribution business. That, of course, is your first step. Part-timers striving for income replacement in order to become full-timers should follow the guidelines of Power Marketers but with more restricted time and longer-term goals. With that exception, part-timers who are seeking to make a little extra income and/or who prefer focusing on product sales should pursue their business according to the plan outlined in this chapter.

Even though there are significant differences in philosophy and style between power and part-time MLM, the first steps are the same, with only a slight alteration.

1. Select the right company.

As in power MLM, a part-timer must use the same criteria to choose a good company before he goes into MLM.

We have already written what these criteria are in Chapter

Two. Go back and read the section on selecting a good company. There is no point in starting from a weak position.

2. Make a list.

An earlier chapter tells how to make this list, who should be on it, and how to contact them. Go back to Chapter Three and read it.

The list, or at least the number of people you contact from the list, need not be as many as for power Marketers. But go ahead and make a full list of everyone you have known so that if you don't get a good response on the first group of people you contact, you won't have to waste time creating another list. You'll have it already prepared.

Part-timers can temper their list phase because there is only a limited number of people you can contact, sign up, and support given the limited time you have decided to spend on MLM.

Once you've made your list, don't spend any time trying to pre-qualify potential candidates or buyers when making your decision. You will probably fail if you do, just as a power Marketer will if he or she tries to prejudge potential candidates.

Here's why. Unless a close friend, family member, or co-worker has already expressed a strong interest in your business or a particular product, there is no way for you to know what turns a person's life has taken. If you are busy prejudging people you haven't seen for awhile but who are on your list, you may be missing a significant group who have made or are willing to make great changes.

For example, if you reread the list phase in power MLM, you will note we instructed people to write down everyone they have ever known. That might even include elementary teachers you haven't seen since you were a child. It happens that some time ago we recruited a young business woman who could only pursue MLM part time. She had horrible results during the initial contacts of her list. We talked and discovered she had primarily contacted co-workers and they, except for one, had rejected her. We suggested that she go farther back in her contacts. So she decided to call her second grade teacher who lived in another state, Missouri to be exact.

Mrs. Lambeth not only remembered her but was delighted to hear from her. Elementary teachers are that way. It turns out that Mrs. Lambeth had retired a couple of years before and was widowed. She had been a very active woman all her life and was going nuts from all the spare time she had. Mrs. Lambeth jumped at the MLM opportunity and is now making over seven hundred dollars a month and is still increasing her production.

From then on, our young recruit has never prejudged whom she should call. You never know when someone is looking for a change, extra money, or has already made a change. What if you have an old acquaintance whose husband was laid off or laid up, but hasn't been in the job market for years and needs or wants to help at home? She might actually need to hear from you.

So don't prejudge your potential recruits. Remember that Ralph Waldo Emerson said that the smartest person he knew was his tailor, because he always measured him anew every time Emerson came in, recognizing we all change daily.

3. Get people to your home and the presentation.

As in the other two steps, there are similarities for the part-time approach and the power approach. That is why it is so important to read both parts. The power approach is bound to help you with ideas, especially on how to approach people. You will not need to focus on cold calls or public speaking so much. However, it is extremely important to get people into your own home to make the presentation.

Here is the most important point to remember in contacting people, getting them to your home, and making the presentation. It happens to be the greatest single difference between the power approach and the part-time product approach. It is also perhaps the part-timer's greatest advantage:

The overriding focus on part-time Multi-Level Marketing is retail sales.

Though part-time Marketers are, of course, concerned with signing up new Associates, the part-timer simply does not have the same time or interest in going on recruiting binges.

Conversely, though a power Marketer has to be concerned with retail sales and product, he has to focus his energy on constantly recruiting to maintain his huge downline.

The part-timer, by both recruiting new Distributors and at the same time building a solid, steady base of customers, can work toward reaching his limited goal and maintaining it. After that point is reached, he can slack off on his recruiting.

This difference in focus on products—their use and sales—directs you in everything you do.

Let's step back to choosing the right company for example. All of our suggestions are important when selecting a good company—things such as how long they have been in business, their marketing plan, their coverage in the area. But to the part-timer, things such as the quality of products, consumption rate, and markup—though important to the power Marketer—will be more important.

It is essential that the products are highly consumable so that customers must reorder. Likewise, there should be a high, though not prohibitive markup. Forty percent is a good standard.

Finally, before you contact anyone, you must use the products you sell and fully believe in their use. You must have a *thorough* knowledge of the products' use and advantages over other products in the marketplace. This is important to your long term success for all sorts of reasons, but the most salient is this: The key to Multi-Level Marketing success is word-of-mouth advertising. This is just as true for the part-timer as it is for the power Marketer. If you use and believe in a product, others around you are sure to want to try it. If it is truly a good product, they will buy it and may be interested in selling it.

All this is a long way of saying that you have the advantage of having not one, but two good reasons to get people to your home:

1. To discuss a good new business opportunity
2. To see a demonstration of some really good and useful products.

These two reasons should cover just about everyone you know. It also takes the pressure off of you to recruit and allows a great deal of flexibility in your presentations. If you find resistance to the business opportunity, all you have to do is switch and convince people to use the products. As long as they become steady users and buyers, you will succeed. This makes much more efficient use of your limited time and effort.

Do not forget your purpose. You are trying to become successful based on a limited goal or goals, spending only small amounts of time. That is why it is essential to find steady users of your products.

The following are some suggestions for making your presentations:

- *Always be prepared and do not speak off-the-cuff.* As suggested in the Power section of this book, very few people are really good at impromptu speaking. Of course, you want to have an easy and laid back demeanor, but you simply must have everything pertinent to your presentation prepared so that you do not fly off on tangents, and so that you give each area you want to cover its proper attention.

- *Disarm people at the presentation by refusing to sign them up in the first interview.* Say something like this: "My intention is not to sign you up at this time. I want you to think about this first and study what I give you."

In addition to the explanation given in the Power section, another reason for using this technique is that you don't want to scare off potential long-term customers by making them feel like they have to be part of your organization to buy the product. Keep in mind your objective: if you can't make the people at your presentation into new Associates in your downline, you can still make them customers.

- *Next, show a video demonstrating both the company's business opportunity and products.* Most good MLM companies are loaded with such video tapes, but be sure you have enough included on the products. They are there for you to use, and we cannot stress enough the importance of their use in enhancing your company's credibility. Also, if you find that the videos are difficult to get from someone in the organization above you, don't be afraid to call the home office.

For some reason, many part-time Marketers are afraid of the company. Don't be. You are as important to them as the biggest producer. They need you because they especially need people who are selling the products on a consistent basis.

- *Next, give a physical demonstration of the products.* Again, most companies have a large supply of material that will explicitly tell you how to do it and will suggest which products best lend themselves to live demonstrations. Some of their instructions may tend to be a little stilted and unrealistic for informal settings, but they can still be useful.

Be creative and stay flexible. It's okay to be a little more formal with strangers than with close friends. Treat this part of the presentation more like a professional clinic, educating people about the benefits of your product line. Put the emphasis on teaching rather than selling by having related professionals give facts, share research, and offer testimonials. Also, don't be afraid to try something new, especially if you have found a better method or more startling way to use a product. Remember that you probably will have a high degree of faith in the product.

Finally, practice the demonstration several times before you try it out on potential buyers or recruits. It's rather embarrassing to have things go wrong with a product demonstration. If the product is supposed to do something, make sure it does it.

- *Explain the company's pricing structure and markups on all the products.* That includes price breaks on large sales. It is possible to do this by using handout copies and going over them with the people.

Do not stop at this point. Create a demonstration to explain how much money a person can make with a certain number of customers who buy on a regular basis. Most companies have the math already worked out to show how easy it is to make good money with only a few customers buying the products.

Do this demonstration on a chalk board, easel, or white board and be prepared to extend the example. Most people still want to know what could happen if their group really takes off. It is also important to stress at this stage of the presentation the percent of the markup that each level gets upon a sale. People will be surprised to see how fast it mounts up.

- *Now that you have the chalk or white board out, it's a good time to illustrate the company's marketing and compensation plans.* Reread this in the Power section of this book. Keep in mind that you need not go into as much detail as is described there. Keep it to a bare minimum, and do not use a grandiose example of how much money people could earn if they had a thousand people in their downlines. Just keep it simple and avoid hype.

Part-Time Exponential Growth Projections

If you plan to pursue your business part time, you might consider this scenario: Your goal is to personally create $100 of volume each month through retailing and personal use combined. You plan to achieve this by the end of your first quarter in the business and teach one other person to do the same. You will probably sponsor a few other people, but only one other will achieve this goal in the first quarter. That doesn't sound too hard—$100 of steady volume in your first three months for you and likewise for one of your Distributors. So by the end of the first quarter, you now have a steady monthly group sales volume of $200 a month. The second quarter, you continue sponsoring a few people, but you are able to find only one other person and teach your Distributor to find one other person to use or share just $100 of product. At the end of the second quarter, you have a total group sales volume of $400. The third quarter you repeat the process, but by the fourth quarter, it starts to break down. So instead of doubling $800 to $1,600, you are only able to reach $1,200 by the end of your first year. You must allow for attrition and human failure. Now continue this process out for another year. Realistically allowing for attrition and people to fail to reach their goals, the second year you reach $10,000 in group sales volume for your whole organization. By now, that generally means that you achieve executive or director level in your compensation plan. The third year you are able to reach $50,000, and the fourth year $200,000. Let's show this process in chart form, remembering that we have allowed for a great deal of attrition and for those people who will not carry on the process.

Volumes	1st Quarter	2nd Quarter	3rd Quarter	4th Quarter
1st Year Volumes	$200	$400	$800	$1,200
2nd Year Volumes	$2,000	$3,500	$6,000	$10,000
3rd Year Volumes	$16,000	$25,000	$36,000	$50,000
4th Year Volumes	$75,000	$100,000	$150,000	$200,000

As you can see, by the end of four years, by using this slow but methodical approach, you have generated over $200,000 of group sales volume, for which, as an executive or director, you are paid handsomely. (To give a conservative estimate, multiply this figure by the percentage or average percentage you are paid on breakaways, generally 2% to 5%.) If you are paid 2% on breakaway executives or directs after four years in the business working part-time, you are now earning an income of $4,000 a month. If you are paid 5%, you are now earning $10,000 a month. You may still have to continue to work with your organization, but part of this income will be passive residual income. Although this hypothetical example took four years to accomplish, you can see the power of exponential growth. Not a bad income for part-time effort! Are you on a track that offers you a better road map in your present j.o.b. (journey of the broke)?

If your plan pays a percentage of gross to the top earners, e.g., 1% of gross shared by those achieving the top level, and if you can see your company reaching $1 million in monthly sales, that represents $10,000 shared by the top earners a month. 1% of $5 million is $50,000 shared by the top earners each month. 1% of $10 million is $100,000 a month shared. 1% of $20 million is $200,000 shared, and 1% of $50 million is $500,000 shared among the top earners. The top Network Marketing companies have achieved this and more. Can you imagine what an additional share of those figures can mean to you if you were able to reach the top of your pay plan and capture your little share of this ... in addition to the rest of your earnings!

If you catch the Network Marketing vision, there are no limits to what you can accomplish with your own independent business, adding people throughout the world to your organization. Your sales compensation plan delivers high leverage without high risk. You aren't required or expected to invest much money with this kind of a program, but you will invest a tremendous amount of your time. It is the hardest work you will ever do, but it only takes your energy and your desire to create your own peace of mind and financial security. For people willing to put forth the effort, the possibility for unbelievable financial returns are here.

For people who can't quite see themselves doing this business in a big way, or lack the confidence to build even as we have described, you may introduce the Millionaires Club as explained on pages 105 and 106. What this does is give people a track to run on, a goal along with a plan for achieving slow but steady success through Network Marketing. And it does this with a product focus which is often more appealing to a part-time person.

- *Follow this with a question and answer period and make sure everyone leaves with literature and some product samples.* That's the best way to end your first discussions of the company and its products.

Almost every company has materials on the company, its success, and powerful testimonials on their products. Get copies from the company. You should never be without them. Pass them out liberally and don't be afraid if some people would like extra copies to give to their friends. Referrals, especially on product sales, are extremely important for part-time Marketers.

Freely give out samples, too, so that even those who don't intend to sell the products might become interested in using them.

Finally, reiterate that you want people to think about whether they would like to become a customer or a member of the organization. You could say something like this: "*You've seen a phenomenal business opportunity and, once you try our samples, you'll see how great the product is. I hope that you will seriously consider joining our organization or, at least, becoming my customer.*"

And don't forget that any customer you create may turn out to be a Distributor in the future, even if they don't seem interested now.

Duplication and Not Deception

Finally, remember how much we have stressed duplication as the combination that unlocks the door to MLM success.

We have found that many part-timers have a tendency to entice their friends into MLM by deceiving them. They often invite friends and acquaintances over for a social evening and then haul out the boards, tapes, and products which usually just makes their guests mad.

We don't think most part-timers are malicious in this, but they just fear rejection and try to stop it before it occurs.

Don't be ashamed of what you are doing or be so afraid of initial rejection that you deceive people. You'll run off most potential recruits and customers and will never accomplish your goals if you get them to your home through deceit. Duplicate the efforts of those who succeeded before you, be flexible, and everything will turn out fine.

Let's review:

- Part-timers striving for income replacement in order to become full-timers should follow the guidelines of Power Marketers but with more restricted time and longer-term goals.

- Like a full-time Marketer, a part-timer must make a list of acquaintances and associates though the list need not be as large.

- When making the list, do not prejudge the people on the list. You can never know their situation. Do not only contact people you've met in recent years. Go back and contact everyone you can.

- Part-timers must get people into their homes for a presentation on the products and the company.

- The overriding focus of part-time product-focused MLM is retail sales.

- By building both a steady base of customers and Distributors, a part-timer can rapidly attain his limited goals.

- Though all the points in selecting the right company are important to both full-time and part-time Marketers, a company's products will weigh more heavily in importance for the part-timer.

- The consumption rate and markup of the products are extremely important to a part-timer. Forty percent is a good standard for markup.

- It is even more critical that part-timers use and believe in the products they sell.

- Here are suggestions for making home presentations:

1. Always be prepared.
2. Disarm people at the beginning of the presentation by refusing to sign them up.
3. Show a video that demos the company's products as well as business opportunity. Be sure enough emphasis is placed on product.
4. Give a physical demonstration of the products, putting the emphasis more on educating your guests than trying to sell them.
5. Explain the company's pricing structure.
6. Illustrate the power of exponential growth, applying your company's compensation plan.
7. Hand out literature and sample product.

• When explaining the pricing structure and compensation plan, use a white board, easel, or chalkboard. Make sure you are prepared.

• Remember that if you cannot convince a person to become an Associate, you can still focus on making them a customer.

• Duplication is the key to success, not deception. Never get someone to your home through deceit.

Chapter 11

Support for the
Part-Time Marketer

You should consider the support aspect of part-time MLM as one of the most essential ingredients to your success. Support is continuous and is more of an ongoing process than the other steps. Remember that strong support is the follow-through to building your organization and client base. It won't get you into business but it certainly will keep you there. Also remember that support, especially close, personal, and regular contact, is much more important to part-time MLM success than it is to power MLM success.

The sheer numbers in power MLM make it impossible to enjoy close personal contact with all people in the downline. A person with a broad frontline and a deep downline has too many people underneath him to help them all personally.

But to a part-timer, each individual in your organization is essential. If you lose a single customer or Distributor, it hurts. If you have only five regular customers, losing one means a twenty percent reduction in income. If you have only five people in

177

your frontline, losing one could mean even a greater reduction in income. Also, given your limited time, it is just too difficult to replace or recruit them.

Finally, part-timers have a tendency to need more direct support and encouragement on an individual basis.

The Three Levels of Support for Part-Time MLM

As a part-time Multi-Level Marketing Distributor you are concerned with three levels of support. They are:

1. Support for yourself.

2. Support for Distributors in your downline.

3. Support for your customers.

Support for yourself

It may sound a little simplistic to include support for yourself here, but that is where people need to begin in order to become successful. We have found, especially among part-timers, that the biggest roadblocks to success are their own attitudes. They often fail before they even give themselves a chance. Too many people quit part-time MLM a mere forty-eight hours to two weeks after they sign up. That is ridiculous. If a person has done his or her homework and selected a good company that has products that are in demand, then he or she has good reason to be in MLM. It is a grave mistake to stop before even starting.

Most people quit or have trouble in part-time MLM for two reasons:

- Fear of rejection or an inability to cope with it.

- Failure to keep motivated and excited about the company's program.

Both reasons feed off of each other though they are subtly different. There are ways to avoid these problems, and for the most part they require thinking and self-talk.

Most people who pursue part-time MLM need a lot more pumping-up and they also have a greater fear of rejection than do people pursuing the power path.

One reason for this is simply the fatigue problem. Excluding retirees, most people in part-time MLM are also pursuing full-time occupations. It doesn't matter if you are a lawyer, mechanic, or homemaker, your work-related interests are more numerous. In the midst of the other work and its problems, it is difficult to focus on making a good effort at MLM. Even if you have some success, the problems have a tendency to overshadow the good, especially if you have problems at work or are handling the endless details of running a home.

On the other hand, we think the limited time you devote to MLM and the fact that each customer or Distributor is more important to your success than in power MLM, will just naturally lead to a fear of rejection. A single rejection means more to you than to someone building a downline of 10,000.

Finally, since a part-timer doesn't face rejection as often as does a power Marketer, he finds it a much more difficult obstacle when it does surface.

What can you do about it? Of course, you can always call your sponsor to talk things out, get suggestions, and air your concerns. We all need support and nurturing. But keep in mind that relying on someone else too much can create a dependency and even exacerbate feelings of inadequacy because someone else is solving your problems. So don't create an over dependency on your sponsor. The best place to start is within yourself.

Here are four suggestions that you can use in your own self-talk which will significantly help you:

1. Review your assets constantly.

We all have a tendency to focus on the things that go wrong or stand in the way of success. But languishing in the mire of problems is an unbalanced approach to life. However bad things appear, you have assets upon which you can build success, so write them down. The list should include the successes you have had so far, the quality of your products, and your personality traits which demonstrate your strengths. Whatever you do, list as many assets as you can, because it is these assets that are the foundation for your success.

2. Review your commitment.

So often people who are in the mire of disappointment, failure, or stagnation have only been going through the motions of doing the work. They have talked a good game but have never really played it.

You have to be honest with yourself and review whether or not you have really put out the effort to succeed. In Network Distribution it doesn't take much hard work, but it does take consistency. More important, it takes smart work and a commitment to do those things necessary to get the job done. That means following the steps and duplicating what others before you have done. If you haven't done so, then you really haven't tried, at least not to the extent that you could possibly reach success.

3. Realize that you may have just had some bad luck.

Let's say you go through a stretch where no one will come to your house for a presentation or several customers decide not to buy for a month or two. Maybe they didn't need more products. There is a good chance that you haven't done anything wrong. These things happen sometimes. It could be just bad luck. After you have reviewed your assets, reaffirmed your commitment and talked to your sponsor, and you still can't find anything wrong, chalk it up to bad luck.

You'll feel better because you'll recognize you're not at fault and that the breaks will eventually turn your way. No matter what the bad luck, don't stop doing what you are supposed to do.

4. Change your thinking about rejection.

Of course it's natural to fear rejection. But work hard on making yourself believe that rejection can be a positive.

We read a study once which stated that a person will say "no" to virtually any sales proposition as many as twenty times before saying "yes." Of course, you probably won't want to ask a person the same question twenty times to finally get a "yes," but don't quit after only a few.

Another tip for handling rejection is to understand that you or the products may be rejected for reasons that have nothing to do with you, your presentation, or the products themselves. It is a fact that if a person invented a product or service that everyone in this country could use, actually needed, and the price was right, some people still wouldn't buy.

There is no way to account for this. It's just that people have all sorts of excuses which they consider valid and refuse to act for a multitude of reasons. You do it, too. So why should it bother you to be rejected when it is as much a part of daily life as breathing and eating?

The most universal fear of rejection evolves because many part-timers believe they are imposing on friends, family, and acquaintances by asking them to buy the products or become Distributors.

If you are selling good products, have a potential of significant added income, and are representing a good company, then what you are offering is a benefit rather than an imposition.

You must believe this. If you are recruiting with a timid mindset, you must convince yourself that what you are doing makes sense. Also, tell yourself that you are doing your friends, family, and acquaintances a favor by presenting the opportunity to them. They may be in the same situation you were in when you decided to become a Network Marketer. They may actually need some extra cash or could be in need of the particular product you are selling.

Support for the Distributors you recruit

The Distributors you recruit need a lot of motivation to make it on a part-time basis.

One thing is critical: *don't necessarily take your clues from the person who recruited you*. Create your own system of support. The person who recruited you may be fine. But too often, once a person's operation is underway, there is a tendency to let Distributors live or die by their own devices.

It's great if your sponsor is supportive. But even if he or she isn't, go ahead and do what it takes to keep your downline motivated.

For the most part, that motivation can come in the form of personal contact and sincere concern. In Power MLM we teach the downline to call up. With a part-time business and smaller organization, for the first few months of a new frontline's career you may want to contact him or her *every two days*. This call doesn't have to be more than an informal, brief chat to find out how he or she is doing. Usually, that is all a person needs. It is nice to know somebody cares. The call also serves to find out if your new Associate has had any problems, to discuss what may be going wrong, and to share new ideas that you have developed that worked for you.

Occasionally, have a coffee get-together at your house with your new Associate or the whole group of Distributors. These get-togethers can be extremely motivating. Remember, many people get into part-time MLM just to get to know other people.

Even if that wasn't a person's primary purpose, you shouldn't overlook the powerful benefits that result from the camaraderie of periodic get-togethers.

Of course, these contacts are good to provide company and product news, including information about larger meetings, motivational tools provided by the company, and contests.

But remember, the most important reason you contact your downline regularly is not to let them know you are alive, but to let them know that you know *they* are alive.

Support for the customer

The most practical point to remember regarding the support for your customers is to keep a good inventory on hand at all times, especially of the products that are moving rapidly and that good customers constantly reorder.

You need not to turn your whole garage into a warehouse as some publications suggest. The tax write-off isn't that great anymore, plus you would have too much money tied up in inventory.

A good rule of thumb to use in stocking inventory is to turn over about 80% of your inventory per month. Consider what you use the most and what runs out the quickest in your home, and then keep an adequate inventory of those items. Keep a couple of month's supply on hand and don't try to stock up for a year regardless of your circumstances.

Don't worry if you don't have a particular product on hand when someone does want to order. It isn't a sin to run out of product and in fact it can be a blessing. It demonstrates the success of your endeavor. If you are close to the customer, he or she won't mind waiting a bit to get it.

That little phrase in the previous paragraph, however—"if you are close to the customer"—is the *real key* to customer support.

You simply must *call your customers regularly*.

You, of course, want to keep in contact with them to see if they need anything else or to tell them of new products by the company or new uses for the products. But the calls are for much more than that. You should try to make your customers your friends.

If your customers are long distance, you may want to use a retail program if offered by your company. In such a program, the company takes their orders on a toll-free order line and, for a nominal fee, will send the product out to your customers. In some cases, an automatic withdrawal program is available, where regularly consumed products can be sent automatically every month and charged, at the request of the customer, to their credit card.

Whether your contacts are near or far, you must always understand that you may be one of the important contacts in your customer's life. We all must remember that the customers are our most important product.

Let's review:

• Support is one of the most essential ingredients to part-time success.

• Close personal support is essential to part-time MLM success. It is more important in part-time than in full-time Network Marketing.

• Part-time Distributors are concerned with support on three levels:
  1. For yourself.
  2. For your downline Distributors.
  3. For customers.

• Support for yourself requires thinking and self-talk. It is important so you can stay motivated and excited about the program and so you can cope with rejection or the fear of rejection.

• Here are four suggestions that you can use in your self-talk:

  1. Review your assets and build on them.
  2. Review your commitment. Be honest and review whether or not you truly have duplicated the program. If not, then you have not commited.
  3. Understand that you may have just had some bad luck. If things have gone wrong for a time but you are committed and doing what you are supposed to, just chalk it up to bad luck. Things will turn around.
  4. Change your thinking about rejection. Think of it as a positive. For every "no" you are closer to a "yes."

• People may reject your products and program for reasons that have nothing to do with you, the program, or the products. All people reject good products for their own personal reasons at some time.

- You must believe in your company and products to the extent that you are doing a favor to your friends and family by letting them in on the opportunity.

- Create your own system of support for your organization. It isn't necessary to follow the system above you.

- For the first few months of a new Distributor's career, encourage them to stay in touch every couple of days. Show that you care.

- Have periodic coffee get-togethers at your home for the whole group. The camaraderie is very supportive.

- The most important reason you contact your downline regularly is not to let them know you are alive, but to let them know that you know *they* are alive.

- In supporting your local customers, you must keep a good supply of products on hand. But don't turn your garage into a warehouse. Keep a supply of those products which are in most demand. Don't worry too much if you run out and have to order. It shows how popular the product is.

- Get close to your customers. Concentrate on being their friend. Call your customers every week.

- For long-distance customers, you may want to use a retail program if offered by your company, whereby the company, for a nominal fee, sends out the product to your customers for you.

- Remember that customers are our most important product.

Conclusion

Our objective in this book was to provide the first definitive work on advanced organizational building. Most of the other books written in the past about our industry were designed for commercial purposes. That is, most authors have attempted to portray an image of Multi-Level Marketing that is a "feel good" approach. However, while those books make success seem easy, they don't actually give one a specific system for building a huge business.

Simply put, most books on this industry have obviously been written to sell books. Thus they have been designed to make everyone feel that they can do this business and that it requires relatively little effort. One author insists that all you need to do is find five good people, then drive their lines deep. Of course what he doesn't reveal is that he's been in 20 different MLM businesses. We've been in one.

Integrity

As a Network Marketer, your success is determined by your ability to access quality training materials, track up line to duplicate the methods of successful leaders who have a proven track record, and build a solid reputation for using ethical recruiting practices. The inherent efficacy of Network Marketing is loyalty to the person who thought enough of you to introduce you to this business. Beware of anyone who tries to persuade you from this philosophy.

Of even greater concern are those who blatantly violate company policy or governmental regulations by such activity as advanced sponsoring or retailing in a new country prior to the company opening there. Verbal networking is legal but product movement or advanced sign-ups are not. Through this kind of dishonorable behavior, such people, though they may approach you first, no longer have earned the right to your loyalty, nor do you want to duplicate this system. Others will attempt to persuade you that you should set aside your allegiance to the Distributor who first introduced you to this business and sign up with them instead. They often lure prospects with promises of having special ties to their company or suggestions that they cannot be successful without local support, and they denounce the inexperience or long distance aspects of working with the person who first introduced you to this opportunity.

The solution cannot be in local support or, as you duplicate the process, you would in turn be forced to develop your business in just one area with no expansion potential. You want to be shown quickly how to become the leader of your organization and not dependent on others for extended local support. The key to our business is in one's ability to teach others a duplicable system for sponsoring and being sponsored from anywhere in the world. Don't try to bypass the person who introduced you, for this person may be inexperienced, but somewhere above them is a person in your upline with the necessary power, income, and experience to work with you and teach you proven techniques for succeeding in this business.

By far, those attracted to Network Marketing are high integrity people who believe in the adage "Do unto others as you would have them do unto you." Commit to this code of honor and this business will serve you well. Beyond the financial and personal freedom possible through this industry are the friendships. We believe in treating each other with the dignity deserving our closest friends. In this business, as in life, what goes around comes around ... for better or for worse.

Duplication

Network Marketing, when practiced in its best form, is a business of simplicity, repetition and duplication. These simple processes, done again and again, are taught to others who do the same processes again and again, teaching others to do the same.

Products are the base of your Network Marketing business, and people are the duplication factor, your way of being able to leverage your time through others. The higher up the pay plan you wish to go, the more balance you'll need in both aspects of business building. You'll want to build a solid foundation based on product sales and consumption; but you'll also want to build a solid organization based on the growth of your Distributor force.

As you duplicate yourself through others, you do so best by example. Be a good role model as a product user, retailer, and sponsor, and show your first level Marketers how to do the business and how to be a good role model for their first level, showing them how to teach their first level to do the same. When you have your second level successfully teaching their first level, thereby reaching down to your third level, you have a solid organization underway!

A word of caution: This business is so different from traditional linear marketing that it is not advisable to begin without some guidance and leadership from those who have gone ahead. Most people who enter this business without prior MLM experience want to translate their skills and areas of expertise into Network Marketing and very often they have some great ideas. But please, do yourself an enormous favor and treat this business like a mini-franchise: follow proven programs of successful leaders and don't try to reinvent the wheel.

Finding Leaders

By now it should be clear that building a large dynamic organization is the most effective way to achieve maximum benefits through the compensation plan. While the general rule is that the majority will join a company for the wholesale benefits of using the product, the next largest group will retail some product, and only a small percentage will choose to build an organization. Those Marketers, though smaller in numbers, will be the source of the greatest portion of your income. The J. Paul Getty theory is exemplified: "I would rather have 1% of the efforts of 100 people than 100% of my own."

You will need to be sifting through a lot of people in order to find the leaders who will allow you to reach to the back end of the sales compensation plan. Ultimate success will be directly affected by your ability to sift. Fight the tendency to prospect only those people who are weaker than you. You may also find it helpful to make a "chicken list" of people who intimidate you. Don't leave any stone unturned in your search for leaders with strong centers of influence. Remember: Leaders are like eagles—they don't fly in flocks but are found one at a time.

You are not necessarily seeking successful people in the traditional sense, but rather people who are doers and, if shown the right vehicle, appear to be the kind of people who could move mountains if that's what it takes to get the job done.

> **"Success is not determined by doing your best but by doing whatever it takes."**
> —*Ralph Waldo Emerson*

Team Effort

Work your plan and your plan will work for you. Be sure that you are operating from a specific plan of action. Don't skip this step. Having set your goals, know exactly how many prospects you must approach every day in order to get the desired number to attend a presentation. Know how many you should be getting to the presentation in order to get the desired number to enroll. Know how many you should be sponsoring in order to get the desired number of breakaways on track to building successful organizations. Work your plan as part of a team effort.

This is a business of team play. Regardless of the background or individual characteristics that we all bring to the business, we depend not only on our own credibility but on that of others. The common thread of successful leaders is their intense drive to achieve and their ability to utilize the power of others. Go upline to find someone successful in this business to lend their credibility to yours. When you first begin, you are not meant to do the business entirely by yourself. As a newcomer, you bring your contacts and your rapport with you; your upline brings experience and a track record of success. The two together can bring phenomenal results.

In the traditional world of business, it is not *what* you know but *who* you know that often brings success. In the world of

Network Marketing, it is not only *who* you know, but who *they* know that builds dynamic organizations.

Enthusiastic Belief

The greatest gift you can give new Marketers is this book. It's an honest appraisal of our industry and a guide to what it takes to succeed. Many people dream of the rewards of becoming a leader in Network Marketing, but relatively few will be willing to pay the price. So by now you realize that this is indeed a work program. This is a legitimate business and in no way a means of getting something for nothing. Those who wait for others to make it happen will fail. It all depends on you. It is your personal power, your consistent and persistent effort that will be the snowflake that starts the avalanche. You have selected your mountain by the company you have chosen. Now begin climbing and don't stop until you reach your peak. Due to varying circumstances, some will reach the top faster than others. The secret is simple: Keep an enthusiastic attitude, never stop recruiting, and just don't quit!

Remember: There are two kinds of people in the world—those who think they can and those who think they can't—and they're both right! We just hope and pray you are among those who think they can. Because if you think you can, you are more than half way to achieving great success in this business.

Thanks for giving us the opportunity to share our concepts with you, and we hope to see you on the beaches of the world.

About The Authors

Mark Yarnell, together with his wife Rene, has built a 100,000-plus member downline since 1986 as an independent Blue Diamond Executive for Nu Skin International. He is well-known for his motivational audio series and public speaking skills. In 1990, he received the American Dream Award from the Howard Ruff Company for parlaying $179 of borrowed capital into an International Network that last year created numerous millionaires and did over $70 million in sales. Mark most recently received the Leadership Award from Upline Financial Press for his contributions to the MLM industry. As a widely respected consultant to the industry, he has been quoted numerous times by the oldest established entrepreneurial magazine in the world: *Success* magazine.

Formerly a minister, Mark enjoys his role as a philanthropist. He is a member of the National De Tocqueville Society, having donated the largest single gift in the history of Nevada to the United Way in Reno. He established and personally funds the only free treatment program in Nevada for alcoholics and addicts, School of Sobriety, now endorsed and utilized by many area judges.

Rene Reid Yarnell achieved Diamond level in Nu Skin International before marrying Mark in 1991. She had built a 4,000 member downline part-time since 1988 while serving in the elected position as County Commissioner in Reno, Nevada. Prior to getting involved in this industry, Rene received her B.A. and M.A. in Theology, having spent four years as a Roman Catholic nun. She produced and hosted her own talk show in radio and television in San Francisco, Denver and Reno. She has been involved in the field of education and owned her own marketing and publishing business.

Rene works with her husband as advocates for the Network Marketing industry. Together, Mark and Rene teach a certification course in Network Marketing at the University of Illinois at Chicago and are two of the founders of the environmentally-concerned International Green Cross of which Mikail Gorbechev is President. Rene serves on the Board of Project ReStart, a program committed to addressing the problems of the homeless in Northern Nevada. The couple resides in Reno, Nevada with their son and daughter who are both currently attending the University of Nevada, Reno.

Additional Books and Training Materials
by
Mark and Rene Reid Yarnell

The Encyclopedia of Network Marketing
200 page guide written by Rene Reid Yarnell
with audio tape series by Mark B. Yarnell
(specify version when ordering)

Should You Quit Before You're Fired?
Great recruiting resource!
Written by noted economics professor Paul Zane Pilzer,
with commentaries by Mark and Rene Reid Yarnell

Power Pack
The book Power Multi Level Marketing
The book Power Speaking
The Video Power Training
Four audio tapes

Power Training Video
Video designed to introduce you into
the world of Networking

The Classic Tapes on MLM
by Mark Yarnell
The ultimate 8-tape series on
how to succeed in MLM

US Sales & Price Info: 800-458-TAPE
8 2 7 3
European Sales & Price Info:
from the US: 800-388-3884
from Europe: 44-181-795-3252